Introduction to Theological German

J. D. Manton

Lecturer in German, University of Technology, Loughborough

© Tyndale Press

39 Bedford Square, London WC1B 3EY

First published October 1971

Second edition January 1973

UK ISBN 0 85111 050 9

USA ISBN 0 8028 1514 6

Library of Congress Catalog
Card Number: 72-94669

Printed and bound in Great Britain by
Weatherby Woolnough Ltd., Wellingborough,
Northants, England.

William B. Eerdmans Publishing Company
Grand Rapids, Michigan

Preface

This course is intended for those who wish to read theological German, but who have little or no previous knowledge of the language.

Experience has shown that there are many students and teachers of theology, as well as ministers of the Christian churches, who need access to German works. Most of the textbooks and language courses available, however, have two major drawbacks from the theologian's point of view: 1. They introduce a wide range of 'everyday' German vocabulary which is not directly relevant to the theologian's needs; 2. they concentrate on promoting oral fluency, which again is not what he is seeking. He therefore tends to expend a great deal of effort in directions which, he hopes, will eventually bring him to his goal, but which, he suspects, do not represent the most efficient path towards it.

The present course is an attempt to meet the theologian's specific need, and to avoid the two above-mentioned drawbacks in the following manner:

1. To concentrate exclusively on religious and theological German; thus almost all the examples in the first ten chapters are drawn from one edition or another of the German Bible, care having been taken to avoid, as far as possible, archaisms of language.

Thus Luther's version has at times been replaced by Das Neue Testament und die Psalmen (Zürich, 1961), which is remarkable for its clear, modern German.

The final ten chapters present passages, gradually increasing in length and difficulty, taken from modern or fairly recent German theological works.

2. To emphasize reading skills rather than oral proficiency, by giving, at the beginning of each of the first ten chapters, a grammatical introduction. This should enable the reader to analyse the texts before him so as to arrive at their precise meaning. In addition, and throughout the whole course, a grammatical commentary is given on each passage, in order to explain difficult points as they occur. These explanations have been kept as simple as possible, though it is assumed that the reader will have an understanding of basic grammatical concepts, e.g. through having studied French or Latin or Greek.

It is important to link a reading knowledge of German with an ability to cope with the spoken word. Fortunately, German is to a large degree regular phonetically, so that an early mastery of the 'Guide to German Pronunciation' (found on pages 6,7) will at least begin to provide this ability. Great help in this direction can be obtained from the various radio and television German series, which would form an admirable adjunct to this course.

Progress can be tested, and useful revision done, by means of the vocabulary lists (up to Lesson XIV). These should be consulted not only when the relevant passage is being studied, but also on a 'retrospective' basis, e.g. at the end of the study of any given chapter, the vocabulary lists of the two previous chapters should be revised. This method will pay handsome dividends in the acquisition of a working vocabulary, and will gradually reduce the recourse which has to be had to the composite vocabulary, and eventually to dictionaries. It is suggested that the English side of the list be covered up; then the German words are read aloud and the English equivalent given.

Words whose meaning is unknown should be marked, then checked over afterwards.

It may well be that students of theology with a particular sphere of interest will find in the course no passage which directly relates to their speciality. None the less, an attempt has been made to introduce as wide a range of theological subject-matter as possible in the last ten chapters, and to include extracts from the works of authors representing a broad spectrum of theological opinion.

I should like to express my indebtedness to the Warden and Librarian of Tyndale House, Cambridge, for the facilities they have granted me in the production of this work.

J.D. Manton
Loughborough, 1970

Books for Further Study

A course of this modest length cannot hope to introduce every German word
which the student of theology will ever meet. The vocabulary found in
this book can be supplemented by the list of 500 German theological
terms with their English translations, together with 500 useful phrases,
compiled by H.J. Siliakus and published by the University of Adelaide
as no. 5 in a series of German Word Lists. A good dictionary, however,
is essential to assist with further reading, and one of the following
may be recommended for this purpose:

Cassell's New German Dictionary. 12th edn (Cassell, 1968).

Schoeffler-Weis Compact German and English Dictionary (Harrap, 1962).
A reference work which is appearing in stages, and which should be completed
during the next few years, is Harrap's Standard German and English Dictionary, Part 1 German-English, edited by Trevor Jones (Harrap, 1963-).

Those wishing to delve more deeply into German grammar should consult,
e.g.

German Grammar for Revision and Reference by F. Clarke (G. Bell & Sons,
1936).

A Manual of Modern German by F.J. Stopp. 2nd edn (University Tutorial
Press, 1960).

A Dictionary of Modern German Prose Usage by H.F. Eggeling (Oxford
University Press, 1961).
It will be found that the books mentioned above will be adequate for understanding any theological German (except the most idiosyncratic!) from Luther
onwards. Any German from the period 1350-1500 should be tackled with the
aid of A. Götze's Frühneuhochdeutsches Glossar. 5th edn (1956).

A Guide to German Pronunciation

For ease of reference, the items in this section are arranged alphabetically. In the case of some vowels, the English 'equivalent' is given with considerable reserve, being at best only a very rough guide. Where there is a French vowel sound which is nearer the German, this is given in brackets. In general, it can be said that a vowel is <u>long</u> if followed by a single consonant within a word, e.g. Vater, Väter, Erlöser; and <u>short</u> if followed by two or more consonants, either finally or within a word, e.g. Gott, Götter, und, unter. The list is not exhaustive, but confines itself to the pronunciation rules exemplified in this course. Examples are given in brackets.
(cf. = compare; Eng. = English; Fr. = French; pron. = pronounced; ⁄ on a German word indicates the stressed syllable and is not part of the normal spelling.)

a   always open; either long as Eng. carter, but with narrower lips (cf. Fr. âne) (Vater), or short as Eng. dash, but with lips further apart (cf. Fr. papa) (das)

ä   (called 'a Umlaut') either long as Eng. care (cf. Fr. père) (Väter), or short as Eng. belt (hält)

au   always long; as Southern Eng. house (Umlaut)

äu   always long; as Eng. boy (Fräulein) (though in names like Matthäus, Irenäus, etc., the ä and the u are pron. as separate syllables)

b   when final, pron. p, but unaspirated (Jakob)

ch   after a, o, u and au pron. gutturally as Scots loch (Bach, Tochter, Buch, auch); otherwise, pron. like h in Eng. huge, only more harshly (ich, euch, Töchter, durch). (In 'Christ', however, and all words derived from it, ch is pron. k)

d   when final, pron. t, but unaspirated (und)

e   either long as Eng. obey, but with narrower lips (cf. Fr. bébé) (der), or short as Eng. dress (es); in unstressed syllables, pron. as Eng. after (Gesetz, Liebe)

ei   always long; as Eng. eye, but with narrower lips (ein)

eu   always long; as Eng. boy (euch)

g   when initial, pron. as Eng. got (gehen); when final, pron. k, but unaspirated (Tag); final ig pron. like German ich (see ch above) (heilig)

h   when initial, always pron. (Herr); after a vowel, not pron. but makes the vowel long (Sohn); between vowels, not pron. (sehen)

i   either long as Eng. see, but with narrower lips (cf. Fr. si) (Elias), or short as Eng. if (bist)

ie   always long; identical with long i above (die)

j   pron. y (Jesus)

k   always pron., even initially before n (Knecht)

o   either long as Northern Eng. boat (cf. Fr. dos) (so, Brot), or short as Eng. got (Gott)

ö   (called 'o Umlaut') either long as ir in Eng. whirl, but with lips pushed further forward (Erlöser), or short, i.e. the same sound shortened (cf. Fr. peu) (Götter)

qu   pron. kv (Quelle)

r	rolled; does not greatly affect previous vowel-sound in mono-syllabic words; after ä, e, eh, i, ie, ih, oh, u, uh, r pron. as separate, very short syllable (Bär, der, lehrt, wir, vier, ihr, Ohr, zur, Uhr)
s	before vowel, pron. z (sie, Sohn); finally, always pron. s (des Lebens)
sch	pron. sh (Schrift)
sp	pron. shp (sprechen)
ss	pron. ss; underlining is used in this course to indicate the special character ß, frequently written either 1. after a long vowel (Strasse); or 2. at the end of a word (dass); or 3. before t (musst)
st	at beginning of syllable, pron. sht (stehen); at end of syllable, pron. as Eng. st (Geist)
th	pron. t (katholisch)
u	either long as Eng. moot (cf. Fr. sous) (gut), or short as Eng. push (und)
ü	(called 'u Umlaut') either long as Eng. eat, but with lips pushed forward to a point (cf. Fr. tu) (Tür), or short, i.e. the same sound shortened (Mütter)
v	pron. f (von)
w	pron. v (was)
y	pron. as ü above; either long (Physiker) or short (systematisch)
z	pron. ts (zu)

Gothic Script

A a	𝕬 𝖆		N n	𝕹 𝖓
B b	𝕭 𝖇		O o	𝕺 𝖔
C c	𝕮 𝖈		P p	𝕻 𝖕
D d	𝕯 𝖉		Q q	𝕼 𝖖
E e	𝕰 𝖊		R r	𝕽 𝖗
F f	𝕱 𝖋		S s	𝕾 𝖘 (ß)
G g	𝕲 𝖌		T t	𝕿 𝖙
H h	𝕳 𝖍		U u	𝖀 𝖚
I i	𝕴 𝖎		V v	𝖁 𝖛
J j	𝕵 𝖏		W w	𝖂 𝖜
K k	𝕶 𝖐		X x	𝖃 𝖝
L l	𝕷 𝖑		Y y	𝖄 𝖞
M m	𝕸 𝖒		Z z	𝖅 𝖟

Lesson I

1. German has three genders: masculine, feminine and neuter. This lesson introduces <u>masculine</u> nouns, whose articles are:

DEFINITE	INDEFINITE
der (= 'the')	ein (= 'a', 'an')

2. <u>All</u> nouns in German begin with a capital letter.

3. The singular (present tense) of <u>sein</u> ('to be') is as follows:

ich bin	I am
du bist	thou art
er ist	he is
sie ist	she is
es ist	it is

VOCABULARY

das ist	that is, this is	der Leib	body
frei	free	mein	my
der Geist	spirit	nicht	not
(der) Gott	God, god	der Sohn	son
der Herr	the Lord	und	and
der Lehrer	teacher	wer	who
		wo	where

SENTENCES

1. Ich bin Gott — I am God

2. Ich bin der Gott Abrahams, und der Gott Isaaks, und der Gott Jakobs (see note <u>a</u> below) — I am the God of Abraham, and the God of Isaac, and the God of Jacob

3. Ich bin Christus — I am Christ

4. Bin ich nicht ein Apostel? Bin ich nicht frei? — Am I not an apostle? Am I not free?

5. Du bist Christus, der Sohn Gottes (note <u>a</u>) — Thou art Christ, the Son of God

6. Wer bist du? Bist du Elias? — Who art thou? Art thou Elias?

7. Du bist mein Sohn (note <u>b</u>) — Thou art my Son

8. Gott ist Geist — God is Spirit

9. Wer ist der Herr? — Who is the Lord?

10. Er ist nicht in Jerusalem — He is not in Jerusalem

GRAMMATICAL NOTES

<u>a</u>. Abrahams; Gottes, etc.

s or es added to a masc. or neut. noun or to a proper name indicate the genitive case (i.e. the possessive form). As in English, proper names in the genitive may either precede or follow the other noun, e.g. Gottes Sohn; or der Sohn Gottes. Names already ending in s do not add another s, e.g. Jonas Sohn (son of Jonas).

<u>b</u>. du

du is used in modern German as the singular, familiar form for 'you' (cf. French, Latin 'tu'), i.e. when addressing one person who is either a relative, or a close friend, or a child. In this course, the archaic forms 'thou', 'thy', 'ye' will be retained in the translations of biblical sentences, since they preserve the German distinction between singular and plural, obscured by the modern forms 'you', 'your'.

FURTHER EXAMPLES

11. Mein Herr und mein Gott!	My Lord and my God!
12. Bist du der Lehrer Israels?	Art thou the teacher of Israel?
13. Adam, wo bist du?	Adam, where art thou?
14. Das ist mein Leib	This is my body
15. Du bist Simon, Jonas Sohn	Thou art Simon, son of Jonas
16. Es ist der Herr	It is the Lord

Lesson II

1. The articles for <u>feminine</u> and <u>neuter</u> nouns are:

DEFINITE	INDEFINITE
fem. die	eine
neut. das	ein

N.B. i. the characteristic final <u>e</u> on the fem. articles.
ii. <u>ein</u> is used before both masc. and neut. nouns.

2. All the possessive adjectives (<u>mein</u>, etc.; see Lesson VII, 4) take
   the ending, if any, which would be on <u>ein</u>, e.g.:

<u>mein</u> Sohn (m.); <u>mein</u> Blut (n.); but <u>meine</u> Mutter (f.)

VOCABULARY

das A und das O	Alpha and Omega	das Leben	life
aus	out of, from	das Licht	light
das Blut	blood	die Liebe	love
dein	thy	die Mutter	mother
das Evangélium (see below)	gospel	siehe!	behold! lo!
das Gesétz (" ")	law	die Tür	door
das Heil	salvation	die Wahrheit	truth
das Lamm	lamb	der Weg	way
		das Wort	word

(Note: an accent on a vowel is not part of the spelling, but in this
course merely serves to indicate the stressed syllable, if different
from English or in an unexpected position. It is also used, in the
course, to eliminate possible doubt as to stress.)

SENTENCES AND PHRASES

1. Ich bin das A und das O — I am Alpha and Omega

2. Ich bin die Tür — I am the door

3. Das ist mein Blut — This is my blood

4. Siehe! das ist Gottes Lamm — Behold, this is the Lamb of God

5. Wer ist meine Mutter? — Who is my mother?

6. Die Liebe ist aus Gott (note <u>a</u>) — Love is from God

7. Gott ist Licht — God is light

8. Das Gesétz Gottes — The Law of God

9. Das Evangélium Christi (note <u>b</u>) — The gospel of Christ

10. Dein Wort ist Wahrheit (note <u>a</u>) — Thy word is truth

GRAMMATICAL NOTES

a. <u>Die</u> Liebe; Wahrheit

   Abstract nouns are often found with the definite article, though usage
   here is not consistent.

b. Christi

   Christus, Jesus and a few other biblical names are sometimes found with
   their original case endings, especially, nowadays, in the genitive case,

e.g. 'die Liebe Jes**u** Christ**i**' ('the love of Jesus Christ')

FURTHER EXAMPLES

11. Ich bin der Weg, die Wahrheit
    und das Leben

I am the way, the truth
and the life

12. Die Liebe Christi

The love of Christ

13. Gottes Wahrheit

The truth of God

14. Der Herr ist mein Licht und
    mein Heil

The Lord is my light and
my salvation

15. Gott ist Liebe

God is love

Lesson III

1. German nouns form their <u>plural</u> in a variety of ways (very rarely with <u>s</u>).
   No attempt to classify them is made here. They are best learnt as they
   occur. In the following vocabulary, the plural form is given in brackets
   after each noun. The plural of the definite article is <u>die</u>; the indefinite article has no plural.

2. The plural (present tense) of <u>sein</u> (cf. introduction 3. to Lesson I) is
   as follows:

wir sind	we are
ihr seid (note <u>a</u>)	ye are
sie sind	they are
Sie sind (note <u>a</u>)	you are

VOCABULARY

aber	but, however	sein	his, its
alles	all, everything	die Tochter (Töchter)	daughter
eins	one	unser	our
der Erlöser (Erlöser)	redeemer	der Vater (Väter)	father
der Gott (Götter)	god	das Volk (Völker)	people, nation
die Herde (Herden)	herd, flock	von	of, from
der Jünger (Jünger)	disciple	der Zeuge (Zeugen)	witness
das Kind (Kinder)	child		

SENTENCES

1. Wir sind sein Volk

We are his people

2. Wir sind die Kinder Gottes — We are the children of God

3. Wir sind seine Zeugen (note b) — We are his witnesses

4. Ihr seid meine Zeugen — Ye are my witnesses

5. Ihr seid Götter — Ye are gods

6. Kindlein, ihr seid von Gott (note c) — Little children, ye are of God

7. Die Töchter sind meine Töchter,
und die Kinder sind meine Kinder,
und die Herden sind meine Herden,
alles ist mein (note d)

The daughters are my daughters,
and the children are my children,
and the herds are my herds,
everything is mine.

8. Ich und der Vater sind eins — I and the Father are one

GRAMMATICAL NOTES

a. ihr; Sie

ihr is used in modern German as the plural familiar form for 'you',
i.e. as the plural of du (cf. Lesson I, note b).
Sie (with capital S) is the polite form for 'you'; it can be used when
addressing either one or more than one person; it always takes a 3rd
plural verb.
This polite form is not used in biblical German, where the only distinction is between du (singular) and ihr (plural).

b. meine Zeugen, etc.

Possessive adjectives followed by a plural noun take the same ending as
the plural definite article, e.g.: die Zeugen; likewise meine Zeugen
deine Zeugen
seine Zeugen, etc.

c. Kindlein

There are two 'diminutive' suffixes: -chen and -lein. It is broadly
true to say that nowadays -chen is the commoner of the two, at least in
standard German. E.g.:

der Sohn	- das Söhnchen (pl. Söhnchen)	little son
die Tochter	- das Töchterchen (pl. Töchterchen)	little daughter
das Kind	- das Kindlein (pl. Kindlein)	little child

N.B. i. All such diminutives are neuter, irrespective of meaning;
    ii.   "   "   "   add Umlaut (") to a,o, or u in the stem;
    iii. "   "   "   remain unchanged in the plural.

d. alles ist mein

The possessive adjectives are often used as possessive pronouns, particularly after the verb 'to be'.

e. wir aber sind

Aber is found either as the first word in a clause (like English 'but'), or inside the clause. Its position does not essentially alter its meaning.

FURTHER EXAMPLES

9. Du bist sein Jünger; wir aber sind   Thou art his disciple; but we
   Moses Jünger (note e above)   are Moses' disciples

10. Du aber, Herr, bist unser Vater und   But thou, Lord, art our Father
    Erlöser   and Redeemer

11. Unser Vater ...   Our Father ...

12. **Herr, du bist unser Gott, und wir**   Lord, thou art our God, and
    sind dein Volk   we are thy people

13. Ihr Töchter von Jerusalem   Ye daughters of Jerusalem

Lesson IV

1. A German adjective always adds an <u>ending</u> when used before a noun,
    whether the noun is actually present or merely understood. The
    ending is determined by the article, etc. which precedes the adjective.
    The scheme of adjective endings is as follows:
    After der (m.), die (f.), das (n.) and eine (f.)   - e
    After ein (m.)   - er
    After ein (n.)   - es
    After all other forms of these articles, including plurals   - en

    (The last section of this lesson contains illustrations of these prin-
    ciples, in the same order as above.)

2. a. Since possessive adjectives before a <u>singular</u> noun behave like the
       indefinite article, adjective endings will be as follows:
       mein geliebt<u>er</u> Sohn (m.); meine geliebt<u>e</u> Tochter (f.); mein geliebt<u>es</u>
       Kind (n.)

    b. Since before a <u>plural</u> noun possessive adjectives behave like the
       plural definite article, adjective endings will be as follows:
       meine geliebt<u>en</u> Söhne; meine geliebt<u>en</u> Töchter; meine geliebt<u>en</u>
       Kinder.

VOCABULARY

(From now on, plurals are indicated in shortened form, by showing in brackets only those elements which are <u>added</u> to the singular, e.g.: der Bund(ü/e) means the plural is die Bünde; der Himmel(-) means the plural is <u>Himmel</u>, i.e. no change in plural.)

alt	old	göttlich (note <u>a</u>)	divine
das Buch(ü/er)	book	gross (note <u>b</u>)	great, big
der Bund(ü/e)	covenant, federation	heilig	holy
		der Himmel(-)	sky, heaven
der Christ(en)	Christian	der Jude(n)	Jew
dies ist	this is	die Kirche(n)	church
die Erde	earth	die Lehre(n)	teaching, doctrine
erst	first	letzt	last
evangelisch	Lutheran	lieb	dear
ewig	eternal	neu	new
das Gebot(e)	commandment	die Schrift(en)	scripture, writing, (literary) work, periodical
der Geist(er)	spirit		
geliebt	beloved		

SENTENCES AND PHRASES

1. Der Herr ist <u>gross</u> (note <u>b</u>)	The Lord is great
2. Der Herr ist ein <u>gross</u>er Gott	The Lord is a great God
3. Dies ist mein geliebter Sohn	This is my beloved Son
4. Ich bin der Erste und der Letzte (note <u>c</u>)	I am the First and the Last
5. Der erste Himmel und die erste Erde	The first heaven and the first earth
6. Ein neuer Himmel und eine neue Erde	A new heaven and a new earth
7. Ich bin der Herr, dein Gott, der Heilige Israels	I am the Lord, thy God, the Holy One of Israel
8. Das aber ist das ewige Leben	But this is eternal life
9. Heilig, heilig, heilig ist Gott der Herr!	Holy, holy, holy is God the Lord!
10. Die göttliche Natur (note <u>a</u>)	The divine nature

GRAMMATICAL NOTES

a. göttlich

The adding of -<u>lich</u> to a noun is a very common method of forming an adjective. If the stem-vowel is <u>a</u>, <u>o</u> or <u>u</u>, Umlaut (") is added, e.g.:

Christ - christlich (Christian)   Liebe - lieblich (lovely)

Geist - geistlich (spiritual)	Mutter - mütterlich (motherly)
Gesétz - gesétzlich (legal)	Natúr - natúrlich (natural)
Gott - göttlich (divine)	Schrift - schriftlich (scriptural)
Kind - kindlich (childlike)	Vater - väterlich (fatherly)
Kirche - kirchlich (ecclesiastical)	Wort - wörtlich (verbal, literal)
Leib - leiblich (bodily)	

b. gross

See note on ss in 'A Guide to German Pronunciation'.

c. der Erste, etc.

Adjectives used as nouns acquire a capital letter.

FURTHER EXAMPLES

(Adjectives with ending -e)

11.	Der Heilige Geist	The Holy Spirit
12.	Der neue Bund	The new covenant
13.	Die heilige Schrift	Holy Scripture
14.	Die evangélische Kirche	The Lutheran Church
15.	Das alte Testamént	The Old Testament
16.	Das erste Buch Mose	The First Book of Moses
17.	Eine neue Lehre	A new doctrine
18.	Seine grosse Liebe	His great love

(Adjectives with ending -er)

19.	Ein kathólischer Theológe	A Catholic theologian
20.	Dein Heiliger Geist	Thy Holy Spirit

(Adjectives with ending -es)

21.	Ein neues Gebót	A new commandment
22.	Unser grosses Heil	Our great salvation

(Adjectives with ending -en)

23.	Die alttestaméntlichen Juden	The Old Testament Jews
24.	Die neutestaméntlichen Christen	The New Testament Christians
25.	Meine lieben Kinder	My dear children
26.	Meine Lieben	My dear ones

Lesson V

1. Most German <u>infinitives</u> consist of stem + <u>en</u>. The endings of the present tense are common to most verbs, and are added to the stem of the infinitive. This stem sometimes shows irregularities in the <u>2nd and 3rd person singular</u>, and very occasionally in the 1st person singular. E.g.:

	GLAUB	EN to believe	HAB	EN to have	GEB	EN to give	WISS	EN to know
ich	glaub	e I believe	hab	e I have	geb	e I give	weiss	I know
du	glaub	st etc.	ha	st etc.	gib	st etc.	weiss	t etc.
er,sie,es	glaub	t	ha	t	gib	t	weiss	
wir	glaub	en	hab	en	geb	en	wiss	en
ihr	glaub	t	hab	t	geb	t	wiss	t
sie,Sie	glaub	en	hab	en	geb	en	wiss	en

N.B. i. Verbs of the <u>wissen</u> type, with irregularities both in endings and stem, are fortunately very few in number.

    ii. Irregularities will normally be indicated by giving the <u>3rd person singular</u> in brackets, e.g. geben (<u>gibt</u>).

2. The following table, showing the accusative and the dative cases of pronouns, is included for reference purposes, since several of these new words occur in the following sentences. The German cases will be explained in Lesson VI.

	<u>ACCUSATIVE</u>		<u>DATIVE</u>	
ich	mich = me		mir = (to) me	
du	dich = thee		dir = (to) thee	
er	ihn = him		ihm = (to) him	
sie	sie = her		ihr = (to) her	
es	es = it		ihm = (to) it	
wir	uns = us		uns = (to) us	
ihr	euch = you		euch = (to) you	
sie	sie = them		ihnen = (to) them	
Sie	Sie = you		Ihnen = (to) you	

<u>VOCABULARY</u>

da<u>ss</u>	that (conjunction)	leben	to live
dieser (m.)	this	lieb haben	to hold dear,
(note <u>c</u>)			to love
geben (<u>gibt</u>)	to give	lieben	to love
glauben	to believe	der Prophét(en)	prophet
die Gnade	grace	sagen	to say, tell
haben (<u>hat</u>)	to have	das Schaf(e)	sheep
halten (<u>hält</u>)	to hold, keep, halt	die Stimme(n)	voice
hören	to hear	warúm	why
kennen	to know (note <u>a</u>)	was	what, that
kommen	to come		(relative)
		wissen (<u>weiss</u>)	to know (note <u>a</u>)
		zu (+ <u>dat.</u>)	to

Lesson V

SENTENCES

1. Herr, ich glaube	Lord, I believe
2. Ich sage euch, ich kenne euch nicht (note a)	I say to you, I know you not
3. Ich weiss, dass du glaubst (note a)	I know that thou believest
4. Hast du mich lieb?	Lovest thou me?
5. Liebst du mich?	Lovest thou me?
6. Herr, du weisst alles, du weisst, dass ich dich lieb habe (note b)	Lord, thou knowest everything, thou knowest that I love thee
7. Alles, was mir der Vater gibt, kommt zu mir	All that the Father gives me comes to me
8. Wir wissen, dass dieser unser Sohn ist (note c)	We know that this is our son
9. Liebt ihr mich, so haltet meine Gebote (note d)	If ye love me, then keep my commandments
10. Sie haben Moses und die Propheten	They have Moses and the prophets

GRAMMATICAL NOTES

a. kennen; wissen

The differences between these two verbs may be broadly summarized
as follows:

kennen (cf. French 'connaître') to know (i.e. be acquainted with)
someone, something

wissen (cf. French 'savoir') to know a fact, to know that ...

b. dass ich dich lieb habe

In a subordinate clause, beginning with a conjunction or a relative
pronoun, the verb is always found at the end.

c. dieser

This word takes the same endings as the definite article, e.g.:
dieser Gott (m.); diese Lehre (f.); dieses Gebot (n.); diese Bücher (pl.)

N.B. -es in neuter, not -as

d. Liebt ihr mich, so ...

i.   Inversion of subject and verb to express 'if ...' is a feature of
German literary style.
ii.   After an 'if' clause, the main clause is often introduced by so.
(Approximate English equivalent, 'then'; often best left untranslated.)

e. Wer ... Christi Geist nicht hat, der ...

i.   Wer not only means 'who?', but may introduce a subordinate clause in
the sense of 'he who ...'.
ii. Der, die, das and die (pl.) may be used as emphatic pronouns, stand-

ing respectively for _er_, _sie_, _es_ and _sie_ (pl.).

<u>f</u>. unseres Herrn
   This is the genitive case (see Lesson I, note <u>a</u>). Herr adds -<u>n</u>, not -<u>s</u>.

FURTHER EXAMPLES

11. Ich weiss, dass mein Erlöser lebt   I know that my Redeemer liveth

12. Ich kenne meine Schafe, und ich   I know my sheep, and I give to them
    gebe ihnen das ewige Leben   eternal life

13. Ich sage euch die Wahrheit   I tell you the truth

14. Wer aber Christi Geist nicht hat, But he who has not Christ's Spirit,
    der ist nicht sein (note <u>e</u> above) he is not his

15. Dein Kind lebt   Thy child liveth

16. Wir haben ein Gesetz   We have a law

17. Ihr kennt die Gnade unseres   Ye know the grace of our Lord
    Herrn Jesu Christi (note <u>f</u> above) Jesus Christ

18. Warum fasten deine Jünger nicht?   Why do thy disciples fast not?

Lesson VI

1. German has four grammatical cases: Nominative, Accusative, Genitive and
   Dative. Their uses are very similar to those of the Greek cases, and
   can be summed up in broad outline as follows:

<u>Nom</u>. Subject/Complement <u>Acc</u>. Direct Object	after certain prepositions	after certain other prepositions to express '<u>motion to</u>...'
<u>Gen</u>. Possession <u>Dat</u>. Indirect Object	after certain prepositions after certain prepositions	after certain other prepositions to express '<u>no motion to</u>..'

2. The <u>definite article</u> declines as follows:

	<u>M</u>.	<u>F</u>.	<u>N</u>.	<u>Pl</u>.
<u>Nom</u>.	der	die	das	die
<u>Acc</u>.	den	die	das	die

Gen.	des	der	des	der
Dat.	dem	der	dem	den

3. The <u>indefinite article</u> declines as follows:

	M.	F.	N.
Nom.	ein	eine	ein
Acc.	einen	eine	ein
Gen.	eines	einer	eines
Dat.	einem	einer	einem

4. The <u>possessive adjectives</u>, as indicated in Lessons II and III, behave like the <u>indefinite</u> article when before a <u>singular</u> noun, and like the plural <u>definite</u> article when before a <u>plural</u> noun.

5. From the principles laid down in Lesson IV, it is clear that any adjective will end in -<u>en</u> following an article, etc. which is:

> masc. acc.;
> <u>gen.</u> or <u>dat.</u> (all genders);
> <u>plural</u> (all cases).

VOCABULARY I

(N.B. From now on, each lesson will contain <u>two</u> vocabulary lists, in order to avoid lists of unwieldy length. The second will be devoted to the 'Further Examples' at the end of the lesson.)

an	at, to (note <u>a</u>)	reden	to talk
auf	on, onto (note <u>a</u>)	das Reich(e)	empire, kingdom
bleiben	to stay, remain	der Richter(-)	judge
der Brief(e)	letter, epistle	Rom	Rome
darum	therefore	der Römer(-)	Roman
durch (+acc.)	through, by (means of)	sei	(may he) be
der Fuss (ü/e)	foot	singen	to sing
der König(e)	king	stehen	to stand
können (ich, er to be able to, 'can'		das Tor(e)	gate
kann; du kannst)		um(+gen.)	for the sake of
das Lied(er)	song	willen	
nehmen (nimmt)	to take	verflucht	cursed
niemand	no-one	von (+dat.)	of, from
		die Welt(en)	world

SENTENCES AND PHRASES

1. Wer den Sohn hat, der hat das Leben; wer den Sohn Gottes nicht hat, der hat das Leben nicht.

   He who has the Son, he has life; he who has not the Son of God, he has not life

2. Niemand, der durch den Geist Gottes redet, kann sagen: 'Verflucht sei Jesus!' (note <u>b</u>)

   No-one who is speaking by the Spirit of God can say: 'May Jesus be cursed!'

3. Er kann nicht in das Reich Gottes kommen (notes <u>a</u>, <u>c</u>)

   He cannot come into (enter) the Kingdom of God

4. Du hast Worte des ewigen Lebens (note <u>d</u>) — Thou hast words of eternal life

5. Um der Wahrheit willen, die in uns bleibt (note <u>b</u>) — For the truth's sake, which remains in us

6. Nimm deinen heiligen Geist nicht von mir! (note <u>e</u>) — Take not thy Holy Spirit from me!

7. Singt dem Herrn ein neues Lied! (notes <u>e</u>, <u>f</u>) — Sing to the Lord a new song!

8. Dein Wort ist ein Licht auf meinem Wege (note <u>g</u>) — Thy word is a light on my path

9. Sie sind von der Welt; darúm reden sie von der Welt, und die Welt hört sie (note <u>h</u>) — They are of the world, therefore they talk of the world, and the world hears them

10. Der Brief des Paulus an die Römer (note <u>j</u>) — The Epistle of Paul to the Romans

11. Das Buch der Richter — The Book of the Judges

12. Das erste Buch der Könige — The First Book of the Kings

13. König der Könige und Herr der Herren (note <u>f</u>) — King of kings and Lord of lords

14. So stehen unsere Füsse in deinen Toren, Jerusalem (notes <u>h</u>,<u>k</u>) — So (shall) our feet stand within thy gates, Jerusalem

GRAMMATICAL NOTES

<u>a</u>. an; auf; in

These are three of the commonest prepositions which can take the accusative or the dative. Other such prepositions are: <u>hinter</u> (behind); <u>vor</u> (before, in front of); <u>über</u> (over; across); <u>unter</u> (under).
If followed by the <u>acc.</u>, they denote 'motion to ....';
" " " " <u>dat.</u>, " " 'no motion to ....'.

Examples:

<u>Acc.</u>	in <u>das</u> Reich Gottes	<u>into</u> the kingdom of God
<u>Dat.</u>	in <u>dem</u> Reich Gottes	<u>in</u> the kingdom of God
<u>Acc.</u>	an <u>die</u> Tür	<u>to</u> the door
<u>Dat.</u>	an <u>der</u> Tür	<u>at</u> the door

<u>b</u>. niemand, der ...; um der Wahrheit willen, die ...

der, die, das and die (pl.) are used as relative pronouns. Their gender and number, of course, are determined by their antecedent. All relative clauses are <u>subordinate</u>, so the verb will be found at the end.

c. Er kann nicht in das Reich Gottes <u>kommen</u>

In a main clause, <u>the infinitive stands last</u>; in a subordinate clause, where the active verb has to be last, the infinitive <u>stands last but one</u>, e.g.: Jesus sagt, da<u>ss</u> er nicht in das Reich Gottes kommen kann.

d. des ewigen Leben<u>s</u>

Most masc. and neut. nouns add -<u>s</u> or -<u>es</u> in the gen. <u>singular</u>; this ending does not appear in the gen. <u>plural</u>, so -<u>s</u> or -<u>es</u> should not be mistaken for a plural.

e. <u>Nimm</u> deinen heiligen Geist; <u>Singt</u> dem Herrn

Since there are in German 3 words for 'you', and since 'you' is the subject (understood) of an imperative verb, it follows that there are 3 different forms of the imperative, depending on who is being addressed:

  i. '<u>DU</u> - form': Sing(e)! Komm(e)! Nimm!
     i.e. the -<u>st</u> of the present tense is removed; optional -<u>e</u> is sometimes found on regular stems.

 ii. '<u>IHR - form</u>': Singt! Kommt! Nehmt!
     i.e. simply the <u>ihr</u> - form of the present tense.

iii. '<u>SIE - form</u>': Singen Sie! Kommen Sie! Nehmen Sie!
     i.e. subject and verb in inverted order.

f. Singt <u>dem Herrn</u>; Herr <u>der Herren</u>

<u>Herr</u> adds -<u>n</u> in all cases of the singular except nom., but -<u>en</u> throughout the plural. N.B. its two other meanings: 'Mr'; 'gentleman'.

g. auf meinem Weg<u>e</u>

Monosyllabic masc. and neut. nouns used in the <u>dat. singular</u> are often found with added -<u>e</u>. This is usually a stylistic device, and has no effect on the meaning.

h. darum <u>reden sie</u>; so <u>stehen unsere Füsse</u>

In a main clause, the active verb is found in the <u>second</u> position. This means that if the clause begins with something other than the subject (e.g. an adverb, as above), then subject and verb become inverted.

j. Der Brief <u>des Paulus</u>

Proper names are frequently found with the definite article, which may be a convenient way of indicating <u>case</u>.

k. in deinen Toren

The <u>dat. plural</u> is distinguished by final -<u>n</u> on article, adjective and noun. Thus, if the nom. plural of the noun does not already end in -<u>n</u>, -<u>n</u> is added in the dat. plural. Here are two other examples:

Nom. pl.: die alten Bücher;   Dat. pl.: in den alt<u>en</u> Büchern
Nom. pl.: diese gro<u>ss</u>en Gebóte;   Dat. pl.: aus dies<u>en</u> gro<u>ss</u>en Gebóten

1. <u>denn</u> das Reich Gottes <u>steht</u> nicht in Worten

Most German conjunctions introduce subordinate clauses (i.e. with verb at end), but <u>denn</u> ('for'), <u>aber</u> ('but'), <u>oder</u> ('or'), <u>und</u> ('and') introduce main clauses (i.e. verb in second position, cf. <u>h</u> above). (The conjunction itself is considered to be merely a link with some previous clause, and is therefore not counted as occupying first position.)

VOCABULARY II

als	as (in the capacity of)	mit (+dat.)	with
denn (note <u>1</u>)	for (conjunction)	die Offenbarung(en)	revelation
dritt	third	rein	pure, clean
die Freiheit	freedom, liberty	sondern	but on the con-
glauben an(+acc.)	to believe in, on		trary (used
jetzt	now		only after a
die Kraft(ä/e)	power		negative)
lebendig	living, lively	die Sünde(n)	sin
machen	to make, do	wandeln	to walk
		zweit	second

FURTHER EXAMPLES

15. Wo aber der Geist des Herrn ist, da ist Freiheit

But where the Spirit of the Lord is, there is liberty

16. Denn das Reich Gottes steht nicht in Worten, sondern in Kraft (note <u>1</u>)

For the Kingdom of God stands not in words, but in power

17. Ihr aber seid der Tempel des lebendigen Gottes

But ye are the temple of the living God

18. Das Blut Jesu Christi, seines Sohnes, macht uns rein von aller Sünde

The blood of Jesus Christ His Son makes us clean from all sin

19. Gnade von Gott, dem Vater, und von dem Herrn Jesus Christus, dem Sohn des Vaters, in der Wahrheit und in der Liebe, sei mit euch!

Grace from God the Father, and from the Lord Jesus Christ the Son of the Father, in truth and in love, be with you!

20. Ich bin das Licht der Welt

I am the light of the world

21. Jetzt aber seid ihr Licht in dem Herrn; wandelt als Kinder des Lichtes

But now ye are light in the Lord; walk as children of light

22. Das Evangelium des Matthäus; (des Markus; des Lukas; des Johannes)

The Gospel of Matthew, etc.

23. Der erste (zweite; dritte) Brief des Johannes

The First (Second; Third) Epistle of John

24. Die Offenbarung des Johannes

The Revelation of John

25. Das ist mein Blut des neuen Bundes

This is my blood of the new covenant

26. Glaube an den Herrn Jesus Christus	Believe on the Lord Jesus Christ
27. Um Christi willen	For Christ's sake
28. Um des Herrn willen	For the Lord's sake
29. Ich bin die Tür zu den Schafen	I am the door to the sheep

Lesson VII

1. The _future_ tense in German is formed very simply, from the present tense of the auxiliary verb _werden_ (du _wirst_; er _wird_) plus an _infinitive_, which of course stands at the end of the clause (see Lesson VI, note _c_).

   N.B. _werden_ also exists in its own right in the sense of 'to become'.

2. Three other _auxiliary verbs_ are also introduced. Like _können_ (see Lesson VI, vocabulary I), they are irregular throughout the singular of the present tense, and they normally require the _infinitive_ of some other verb to complete the sense. They are:

müssen (ich, er muss; du musst)	to have to; 'must'
sollen (ich, er soll; du sollst)	to be supposed to; 'shall' (in questions, promises, commands, warnings, etc.)
wollen (ich, er will; du willst)	to want to; intend to; be willing to

3. Verbs whose infinitive has a prefix are of two kinds:

   a. _separable_ (marked 'sep.' in vocabulary), i.e. the prefix is _stressed_ in pronunciation, and in a main clause or a question separates from the active verb and is found at the end, e.g. ausgehen, 'der Geist geht vom Vater _aus_', the Spirit proceeds from the Father. In sentence 3 (below), this verb appears unseparated, because it is in a relative (i.e. subordinate) clause, not a main clause. See Lesson V, note _b_.

   b. _inseparable_ (marked 'insep'. in vocabulary), i.e. the prefix is _unstressed_ in pronunciation and never separates from the verb, e.g. vergehen: 'meine Worte _vergehen_ nicht', my words do not pass away. The following prefixes are always inseparable: be-, emp-, ent-, er-, ge-, miss-, ver-, zer-.

English readers of German have to acquire the habit of looking ahead to the end of the clause, since so many important things congregate there! In the case of separable verbs, it is essential to find the prefix, (a) because it almost always affects the meaning of the verb; (b) because if the infinitive has to be looked up in a dictionary, it will be given there with the prefix first.

4. The complete list of <u>possessive adjectives</u> is as follows:

(ich)	mein	('my')
(du)	dein	('thy')
(er, es)	sein	('his', 'its')
(sie)	ihr	('her')
(wir)	unser	('our')
(ihr)	euer	('your')
(sie)	ihr	('their')
(Sie)	Ihr	('your')

VOCABULARY I

		jemand	someone, anyone
án/klopfen (sep.)	to knock		
die Arbeit	work	kein (like poss.	not a, no,
auch	also, even	adjectives)	not any
die Auferstehung	resurrection	lassen (du, er lässt)	to leave, let,
áuf/tun (sep.)	to open		allow, cause
áus/gehen (sep.)	to go out, proceed	das Mahl(e)	meal
der Beistand	assistance, helper	noch	still, yet, nor
		sein (infinitive)	to be
		stehlen (stiehlt)	to steal
die Ewigkeit	eternity	sterben (stirbt)	to die
der Friede (note b)	peace	vergehen (insep.)	to pass away
gehen	to go	wenn	when, whenever, if
hinéin/gehen (sep.)	to go in		
		wohín	whither
jeder (like <u>def.</u> article)	each, every (one)	zeugen	to testify, bear witness

SENTENCES

(No English translations will be given from now on; difficult phrases will be translated in the grammatical notes.)

1. Ich werde zu euch kommen. (Jn. 14:18)

2. Herr, wohín sollen wir gehen? (Jn. 6:68)

3. Wenn aber der Beistand kommt, den ich euch vom Vater senden werde, der Geist der Wahrheit, der vom Vater áusgeht, der wird von mir zeugen, und ihr werdet auch zeugen. (note <u>a</u>) (Jn. 15:26,27)

4. Frieden lasse ich euch, meinen Frieden gebe ich euch. (note <u>b</u>) (Jn. 14:27)

5. Siehe, ich stehe vor der Tür und klopfe án. Wenn jemand meine Stimme hört und die Tür áuftut, werde ich zu ihm hinéingehen und das Mahl mit ihm halten, und er mit mir. (note <u>c</u>) (Rev. 3:20)

6. Himmel und Erde werden vergehen; meine Worte aber werden nicht vergehen. (Mt. 24:35)

7. Du sollst nicht stehlen. (Ex. 20:15)

8. Am Sabbath sollst du keine Arbeit machen, noch dein Sohn, noch deine Tochter. (note a) (Ex. 20:10)

9. Jesus sagt zu ihr: 'Ich bin die Auferstehung und das Leben; wer an mich glaubt, der wird leben, auch wenn er stirbt, und jeder, der lebt und an mich glaubt, wird in Ewigkeit nicht sterben. Glaubst du das?' (Jn. 11:25,26)

10. Ihr sollt heilig sein, denn ich bin heilig, der Herr, euer Gott. (Lv. 19:2)

11. Wenn ihr meine Gebote haltet, bleibt ihr in meiner Liebe. (note c) (Jn. 15:10)

12. Wollt ihr auch seine Jünger werden? (Jn. 9:27)

GRAMMATICAL NOTES

a. **vom** Vater; **am** Sabbath

The following abbreviations are very common :
vom = von dem; am = an dem; ans = an das; beim = bei dem; im = in dem; ins = in das; zum = zu dem; zur = zu der

b. Frieden lasse ich euch; Der Menschensohn

i. A handful of masc. nouns whose nom. singular ends in -e add -ns in the gen. singular, and -n in all other cases, singular and plural. Two similar examples occur in the Further Examples below: der Glaube; der Name.

ii. Mensch adds -en in all cases singular and plural, except nom. singular. It belongs to a fairly large group of masc. nouns denoting living beings which add -n or -en in declension.

c. Wenn jemand ... auftut, werde ich ...; Wenn ihr ... haltet, bleibt ihr

In a main clause, inversion of subject and verb occurs not only after some initial word or phrase which is not the subject (see Lesson VI, note h), but also after a subordinate clause.

d. von sich ('of himself')

Sich may be described as the all-purpose reflexive pronoun of the 3rd person, both singular and plural. (The 1st and 2nd persons have reflexive pronouns identical with acc. and dat. of their ordinary personal pronouns, see list in Lesson V). N.B. German reflexive pronouns can be used both after verbs, e.g. er liebt sich; and after prepositions, e.g. er redet von sich.

e. von sich selbst

Selbst can be used, for emphasis, with any person, singular or plural

(cf. French 'même' in 'lui-même'), e.g.:
ich selbst ('I myself'); er selbst ('he himself'); wir selbst ('we our-
selves'); Gott selbst ('God Himself').

f. ... der Glaube ..., ist er tot

er, sie and es may all mean 'it', depending on the gender of the noun
referred to.

VOCABULARY II

auf/erstehen (sep.)	to rise again (from dead)
bei (+ dat.)	with, at the house of (cf. French 'chez')
der Bruder(ü)	brother
der Glaube (note b)	faith, belief
jener (like def. article)	that (one)
leiden	to suffer
leiten	to direct, conduct
der Mensch (note b)	human being, person
der Menschensohn (or: des Menschen Sohn)	Son of man
der Name (note b)	name
selbst (note e)	-self
tot	dead
tun (du tust; er tut)	to do
unter (see Lesson VI, note a)	under, among
viel	much
das Werk(e)	(piece of) work
wie	how; like, as
wohnen	to dwell
die Wohnung(en)	dwelling, flat
das Zeichen(-)	sign
zeigen	to show

FURTHER EXAMPLES

13. Ich will unter ihnen wohnen und unter ihnen wandeln, und ich will ihr
    Gott sein, und sie sollen mein Volk sein. (2 Cor. 6:16)

14. Wer mich liebt, der wird mein Wort halten; und mein Vater wird ihn lieben,
    und wir werden zu ihm kommen und Wohnung bei ihm machen. Wer aber mich
    nicht liebt, der hält meine Worte nicht. Und das Wort, das ihr hört, ist
    nicht mein, sondern des Vaters. (Jn. 14:23,24)

15. Wenn aber jener kommt, der Geist der Wahrheit, der wird euch in alle
    Wahrheit leiten. Denn er wird nicht von sich selbst reden, sondern
    was er hört, das wird er reden. (notes d, e) (Jn. 16:13)

16. Dein Bruder soll auferstehen. (Jn. 11:23)

17. Wenn der Glaube nicht Werke hat, ist er tot. (note f) (Jas. 2:17)

18. Der Menschensohn muss viel leiden. (note b) (Mk. 8:31)

19. Ich will ihm zeigen, wieviel er um meines Namens willen leiden muss.
    (Acts 9:16)

20. Niemand kann die Zeichen tun, die du tust. (Jn. 3:2)

21. Er wird bei ihnen wohnen, und sie werden sein Volk sein, und Er selbst,
    Gott mit ihnen, wird ihr Gott sein. (Rev. 21:3)

22. Herr, was willst du, dass ich tun soll? - Ich werde dir sagen, was du
    tun sollst. (Acts 9:6)

Lesson VIII

This lesson and the next introduce the main German past tenses.

IMPERFECT

This is the simple past tense and covers:

> single action (e.g. I went);
> continuous action (e.g. I was going);
> repeated action (e.g. I used to go).

The following table shows the imperfect of a 'weak' (i.e. regular) verb, and
of several important 'strong' (i.e. irregular) verbs.

	WEAK			STRONG					
	SAG|EN 'to say'			NEHM|EN 'to take'		GEH|EN 'to go'		SEIN 'to be'	
ich	sag	te	I said,	nahm|-	I took,	ging|-	I went,	war|-	I was,
du	sag	test	etc.	nahm|st	etc.	ging|st	etc.	war|st	etc.
er,sie,es	sag	te		nahm|-		ging|-		war|-	
wir	sag	ten		nahm|en		ging|en		war|en	
ihr	sag	tet		nahm|t		ging|t		war|t	
sie,Sie	sag	ten		nahm|en		ging|en		war|en	

N.B. i. The characteristic -t- in the endings of weak verbs. (Weak verbs
whose stems end in -d or -t insert -e- before imperfect endings,
e.g. ich antwortete.)

ii. Strong verbs are without this -t-; in the stem they invariably
show a change, which may involve a single letter (e.g. nahm), or
may be more radical (e.g. ging; war).

iii. A few verbs, which we shall call 'irregular weak', have weak
endings <u>and</u> a change in the stem. Some of the most important are:

<u>haben</u>	'to have'	: ich	<u>hatte</u>
<u>werden</u>	'to become'	: ich	<u>wurde</u>
<u>müssen</u>	'to have to'	: ich	<u>musste</u>
<u>können</u>	'to be able to'	: ich	<u>konnte</u>
<u>nennen</u>	'to call, name'	: ich	<u>nannte</u>
<u>kennen</u>	'to know'	: ich	<u>kannte</u>
<u>wissen</u>	'to know'	: ich	<u>wusste</u>

<u>VOCABULARY I</u> (Strong or irregular <u>imperfects</u> occurring in the passages below
are indicated by the <u>3rd</u> person sing. in brackets)

der Abend(e)	evening	schaffen (<u>schuf</u>)	to create
der Anfang(ä/e)	beginning	scheiden (<u>schied</u>)	to divide,
da	there, then		separate
dazú	in addition	schweben	to hover
finster	dark	sehen (<u>sah</u>)	to see
die Finsternis	darkness	sprechen (<u>sprach</u>)	to speak
gut	good	der Stern(e)	star
klein	small	der Tag(e)	day
leer	empty	die Tiefe(n)	the deep; depth
der Morgen(-)	morning	das Wasser	water
die Nacht(ä/e)	night	wüst	desolate, waste
nennen (<u>nannte</u>)	to name, call	zwei	two
regíeren	to rule		

FIRST PASSAGE

Am Anfang schuf Gott den Himmel und die Erde. Und die Erde war wüst und
leer, und es war finster auf der Tiefe; und der Geist Gottes schwebte auf
dem Wasser. Und Gott sprach (note <u>a</u>): 'Es werde Licht!' (note <u>b</u>) Und es
wurde Licht. Und Gott sah, dass das Licht gut war. Da schied Gott das
Licht von der Finsternis, und nannte das Licht Tag, und die Finsternis
Nacht. Da wurde aus Abend und Morgen der erste Tag.
Und Gott machte zwei <u>grosse</u> Lichter (note <u>c</u>): ein <u>grosses</u> Licht, das
den Tag regíeren sollte, und ein kleines Licht, das die Nacht regíeren
sollte, dazú auch die Sterne. (Gn. 1:1-5,16)

GRAMMATICAL NOTES

<u>a</u>. Und Gott <u>sprach</u>
This use of <u>sprechen</u> in the sense of 'to say' has a distinctly biblical
ring, and is retained here because the sublimity of the style seems to
require it. Normal modern usage would demand <u>sagte</u>.

<u>b</u>. Es <u>werde</u> Licht! (literally: 'let it become light!')
<u>Werde</u> is present subjunctive (dealt with in Lesson X), and is used here
to express a <u>wish</u>. <u>Sei</u> (see Lesson VI) is also present subjunctive and
expresses the wish 'let (him, it) be', 'may (he, it) be'.

<u>c</u>. Gott machte zwei <u>grosse</u> Lichter
An adjective before a noun, but without a preceding article, possessive
adjective, etc., takes the ending which would have been on the <u>definite
article</u> had one been present. In the sentence above, <u>Lichter</u> is acc.
plural, so the definite article would have been <u>die</u>.

d. Jona <u>zu</u> verschlingen

    In sentences, the infinitive is regularly found with <u>zu</u>, except after
the auxiliary verbs <u>können</u>, <u>müssen</u>, <u>sollen</u>, <u>werden</u>, <u>wollen</u> and one or
two others. If the infinitive is separable, <u>zu</u> is inserted between
prefix and stem, and the whole is written as one word, e.g.: ánzuklopfen;
hinéinzugehen.

VOCABULARY II

die Angst	fear	mitten in (+<u>dat.</u>)	in the midst of
antworten (+<u>dat.</u>)	to answer	rufen (<u>rief</u>)	to call, shout
der Bauch(åu/e)	belly	schreien (<u>schrie</u>)	to cry, yell
beten	to pray	umgében (insep.)	to surround
drei	three	(<u>umgáb</u>)	
der Fisch(e)	fish	verscháffen (insep.)	to provide, supply
die Flut(en)	flood, high	verschlíngen (insep.)	to swallow up
	tide die Welle(n)		wave
die Hölle	hell	werfen (<u>warf</u>)	to throw, cast
das Meer(e)	sea	die Woge(n)	billow

SECOND PASSAGE

    Aber der Herr verscháffte einen grossen Fisch, Jona zu verschlíngen.
(note <u>d</u>)   Und Jona war im Bauche des Fisches drei Tage und drei Nächte. Und
Jona betete zu dem Herrn, seinem Gott, im Bauche des Fisches, und sagte:
'Ich rief zu dem Herrn in meiner Angst, und er antwortete mir; ich schrie
aus dem Bauch der Hölle, und du hörtest meine Stimme. Du warfst mich in
die Tiefe mitten im Meer, dass die Fluten mich umgáben; alle deine Wogen
und Wellen gingen über mich.' (Jon. 2:1-4)

Lesson IX

This lesson continues the treatment of <u>past tenses</u> begun in Lesson VIII.

1. PERFECT

As in English, this is a compound tense, formed from an auxiliary verb
(usually <u>haben</u>, sometimes <u>sein</u>) plus the <u>past participle</u>.
<u>Weak</u> past participles are formed thus:

    ge<u>sagt</u>, e.g. Ich habe gesagt ('I have said')
    ge<u>antwortet</u>, e.g. Ich habe geantwortet ('I have answered')

Strong past participles are formed thus:

genommen	(from nehmen	'to take')
gegangen	(from gehen	'to go')
gewesen	(from sein	'to be')
gesprochen	(from sprechen	'to speak')
gegeben	(from geben	'to give')

N.B. i. Past participles usually begin with ge-.
    ii. Weak (and 'irregular weak') past participles have the characteristic ending -t (cf. weak imperfects, Lesson VIII).
   iii. Strong past participles end in -en, and may or may not show a change in stem.

2. PLUPERFECT

This tense is formed from the imperfect of the auxiliary, plus the past participle, e.g.:

    ich hatte gesagt   'I had said'
    ich hatte gesprochen   'I had spoken'

3. The same rules of word order apply to the past participle as to the infinitive, i.e.:
in a main clause, the past participle stands last;
in a subordinate clause, the past participle stands last but one, with the auxiliary verb last.

VOCABULARY I

(N.B. those strong past participles occurring in the passages below are indicated in brackets after the abbreviation p.p. Stress is not indicated on p.p.s beginning with ge-, since it invariably falls on the next syllable, i.e. on the verb stem.

behérbergen (insep.)	to shelter, take in
bekléiden (insep.)	to clothe
besúchen (insep.)	to visit
dann	then
durstig	thirsty
essen	to eat
die Frau(en)	woman, wife, Mrs.
fremd	strange, unfamiliar, foreign
fünf	five
geben (p.p. gegeben)	to give
das Gefängnis(se)	prison
gerécht	just, fair, righteous
gering	unimportant, meagre
hungrig	hungry
kommen (p.p. gekommen) (note a)	to come
krank	ill, sick
der Mann(ä/er)	man, husband
nackt	naked
das Recht(e)	law, right, rectitude
sehen (p.p. gesehen)	to see
sein (p.p. gewesen) (note a)	to be

Lesson IX

tränken	to give drink to
tun (p.p. _getan_)	to do
wahrlich	truly, verily
wann?	when?

FIRST PASSAGES

1. Die Frau antwortete und sagte zu ihm: 'Ich habe keinen Mann.' Jesus
sagte zu ihr: 'Du hast mit Recht gesagt: "Ich habe keinen Mann", denn
fünf Männer hast du gehabt, und der, den du jetzt hast, ist nicht
dein Mann; da hast du die Wahrheit gesagt.' (Jn. 4:17,18)

2. 'Ich bin hungrig gewesen (note _a_), und ihr habt mir zu essen gegeben.
Ich bin durstig gewesen, und ihr habt mich getränkt. Ich bin fremd
gewesen, und ihr habt mich beherbergt (note _b_). Ich bin nackt
gewesen, und ihr habt mich bekleidet. Ich bin krank gewesen, und
ihr habt mich besucht. Ich bin im Gefängnis gewesen, und ihr seid
zu mir gekommen' (note _a_).

Dann werden ihm die Gerechten antworten und sagen: 'Herr, wann haben
wir dich hungrig gesehen, und haben dir zu essen gegeben? oder durstig, und haben dich getränkt? Wann haben wir dich als Fremden
gesehen, und beherbergt? Wann haben wir dich krank oder im Gefängnis
gesehen, und sind zu dir gekommen?' Und der König wird antworten und
zu ihnen sagen: 'Wahrlich, ich sage euch: was ihr einem (note _c_) unter
diesen meinen geringsten Brüdern (note _d_) getan habt, das habt ihr mir
getan.' (Mt. 25:35-40)

GRAMMATICAL NOTES

_a_. Ich _bin_ hungrig gewesen; ihr _seid_ zu mir gekommen

The following verbs form their perfect and pluperfect tenses not with
haben but with _sein_:

i. _sein_ itself (see above); _bleiben_ 'to remain': er _ist_ geblieben
ii. _intransitive_ verbs denoting a _change of place_, e.g.:
    kommen 'to come' (see above)
    gehen 'to go': er _ist_ gegangen
iii. _intransitive_ verbs denoting a _change of state_, e.g.:
    sterben 'to die': er _ist_ gestorben
    werden 'to become': er _ist_ geworden

_b_. Ihr habt mich beherbergt

Inseparable verbs form their past participles without _ge-_.

_c_. einem ('to one')

i. The ordinary word for the number 'one' is _eins_. However, 'one man'
is _ein_ Mann; 'one woman' is _eine_ Frau; 'one child' is _ein_ Kind;
i.e. 'one' before a noun is identical with the indefinite article,
though in print it may be distinguished by italics or spaced type,
and in speech will probably be stressed.

ii. The _pronoun_ 'one' (as here) is _einer_ (masc.); _eine_ (fem.); _eines_
(neut.), which declines like the _definite_ article; _einem_ (above)
is masc. dat.

d. unter diesen meinen geringsten Brüdern (literally: 'among these my most unimportant brethren').

German adjectives form their comparative and superlative as follows:

klein:	kleiner (smaller);	kleinst-(smallest)
alt:	älter (older);	ältest-(oldest)
intelligént:	intelligénter (more intelligent);	intelligéntest-(most intelligent)

N.B. i. these forms all add normal adjective endings when before nouns or when used as nouns; the superlative must always have an adjective ending, i.e. it is never found in the 'bald' form given above.

ii. many monosyllabic adjectives (e.g. alt, above) with stem-vowel a, o or u add Umlaut (") in comparative and superlative.

iii. the number of syllables does not affect the formation of the comparative and superlative as it does in English (e.g. intelligent, above)

iv. the two most important exceptions to the scheme given above are:
gut: besser (better); best- (best)
viel: mehr (indeclinable)(more); meist- (most).

e. Wer hat dem Menschen den Mund geschaffen?

Der Mensch is frequently used in the singular in the generic sense of 'man', 'mankind'. Here it is dat. singular, being the indirect object; literally: 'Who has created the mouth for man?'

f. Sehenden

Present participles are formed by adding -d to infinitives. They are hardly ever used as verbs, almost always as adjectives. In the example above, the final -en is the normal masc. acc. singular adjective ending. All the adjectives in the sentence concerned are used as nouns, hence the capital letters (see Lesson IV, note c).

g. Eure Väter

Whenever an ending is added to euer (see Lesson VII, Introduction), the second -e drops out.

h. fünfundsiebzig (literally: 'five and seventy')

i. Practically any German number can be worked out if the following are known:

1	eins	11	elf	100	hundert
2	zwei	12	zwölf	1,000	tausend
3	drei	13	dreizehn	1,000,000	eine Millión
4	vier	14	vierzehn etc.		
5	fünf				
6	sechs	20	zwanzig		
7	sieben	22	zweiundzwanzig		
8	acht	30	dreissig		
9	neun	40	vierzig etc.		
10	zehn				

ii. The ordinal numbers 1st, 2nd and 3rd were dealt with in Lessons IV and VI. These are, of course, adjectives, so take ordinary adjective endings.

The ordinals 4th to 19th add -t to the cardinal number, e.g. der zehnte,
'the 10th'
"   "   20th to 100th add -st " "   "   "   e.g. der fünfund-
achtzigste, 'the 85th'

j. als er aus Haran zog

The uses of the three words for 'when' may be summed up as follows:

i. als - single activity in the past (e.g. above)
ii. wann - question, either direct (e.g. in Passage 2 of this lesson,
second paragraph) or indirect, e.g. Ich weiss nicht, wann
er kommt.
iii. wenn - in all other senses, including 'whenever':
Wenn er kommt, sagen Sie es mir ('When he comes, tell me')
Wenn er kam, sagte er nichts ('Whenever he came, he used to say
nothing')

N.B.   Wenn also means 'if' (see Lesson VII)

VOCABULARY II

(N.B. strong imperfects occurring in the sentences below are indicated by
the abbreviation imp.; strong past participles by p.p.)

als	when (note j)
also	so, therefore
áus/ziehen (sep.)	to move out, go out
(imp. zog)	
bauen	to build
das Brot	bread, loaf
erschéinen (insep.)	to appear
(p.p. erschíenen)	
erwérben (insep.)	to gain,
(p.p. erwórben)	acquire
essen (p.p. gegessen)	to eat
fünfundsiebzig (note h)	seventy-five
gewínnen (insep.)	to win, gain
(p.p. gewónnen)	
die Habe	property
das Jahr(e)	year
das Land(ä/er)	land, country, countryside, state (e.g. in Federal Republic of Germany)
der Mund	mouth
nehmen (imp. nahm)	to take
reisen	to travel, journey
schaffen	to create
(p.p. geschaffen)	
schreiben	to write
(p.p. geschrieben)	
die Seele(n)	soul
sterben	to die
(p.p. gestorben)	
stumm	dumb
taub	deaf
um ... zu (+infinitive)	in order to ...
die Wüste	desert, wilderness
ziehen (imp. zog)	(transitive) to pull (intransitive) to move, to go

FURTHER EXAMPLES

3. Was ich geschrieben habe, das habe ich geschrieben. (Jn. 19:22)

4. Der Herr sagte zu ihm: 'Wer hat dem Menschen (note e) den Mund geschaffen? Oder wer hat den Stummen oder Tauben oder Sehenden (note f) oder Blinden gemacht? Habe Ich es nicht getan, der Herr?' (Ex. 4:11)

5. Eure Väter (note g) haben in der Wüste das Manna gegessen und sind gestorben ... Ich bin das lebendige Brot, das vom Himmel gekommen ist. (Jn. 6: 49,51)

6. Da zog Abram aus, wie der Herr zu ihm gesagt hatte, und Lot zog mit ihm. Abram war fünfundsiebzig (note h) Jahre alt, als (note j) er aus Haran zog. Also nahm Abram seine Frau Sarai und Lot, den Sohn seines Bruders, mit aller ihrer Habe, die sie gewonnen hatten, und die Seelen, die sie in Haran erworben hatten, und sie zogen aus, um in das Land Kanaan zu reisen ... und er baute da einen Altar dem Herrn, der ihm erschienen war. (Gn. 12:4,5,7)

Lesson X

In certain circumstances, German verbs appear in special forms known as subjunctives. Basically, there are two tenses of the subjunctive: present and imperfect (for compound tenses, see paragraph 3 below)

1. The PRESENT SUBJUNCTIVE

This has the following main uses:

a. in the sense of 'let it ...', 'may he ...', etc., i.e. expressing a wish or a supposition;

b. in reported speech.

It is formed from the stem of the infinitive, as follows:

	MACH	EN 'to make'	SPRECH	EN 'to speak'	MÜSS	EN 'to have to'
ich	mach	e	sprech	e	müss	e
du	mach	est	sprech	est	müss	est
er,sie,es	mach	e	sprech	e	müss	e
wir	mach	en	sprech	en	müss	en
ihr	mach	et	sprech	et	müss	et
sie,Sie	mach	en	sprech	en	müss	en

N.B. i. Endings are identical for all verbs, weak or strong. Strong and 'irregular weak' verbs have no change in the stem.

ii. The one crucial exception:

	SEI	N	'to be'
ich	sei	-	
du	sei	est	
er,sie,es	sei	-	
wir	sei	en	
ihr	sei	et	
sie,Sie	sei	en	

2. The IMPERFECT SUBJUNCTIVE

This has the following main uses :

a. in conditional ('if') sentences, as in English sentences of the type: 'if I were rich ...';

b. in the sense of 'would'/'could'/'should';

c. in reported speech.

It is formed from the stem of imperfect tense, as follows:

MACHEN		SPRECHEN		MÜSSEN	
(imperfect stem: macht-)		(imperfect stem: sprach-)		(imperfect stem: musst-)	
ich	macht e	spräch	e	müsst	e
du	macht est	spräch	est	müsst	est
er,sie,es	macht e	spräch	e	müsst	e
wir	macht en	spräch	en	müsst	en
ihr	macht et	spräch	et	müsst	et
sie, Sie	macht en	spräch	en	müsst	en

N.B. i. the imperfect subjunctive of weak verbs is identical with their ordinary imperfect.

ii. strong and 'irregular weak' verbs add Umlaut ("), where possible, to the stem;

iii. endings are identical with those of the present subjunctive, and are the same for all verbs, including sein, which therefore goes:

SEIN

(imperfect stem: war-)

ich wär | e
du wär | est
etc.

The imperfect subjunctive sometimes sounds pedantic, so is often avoided by the simpler construction: würde ('would', 'should') plus the infinitive, e.g.:

ich würde machen,	instead of	ich machte
du würdest sprechen,	" "	du sprächest
er würde gehen,	" "	er ginge
wir würden sehen	" "	wir sähen

etc.

(Würde is itself the imperfect subjunctive of 'werden'.)

3. COMPOUND TENSES OF THE SUBJUNCTIVE

These are formed quite simply, by changing the <u>auxiliary</u> verb into the present or imperfect subjunctive, as appropriate, thus:

FUTURE	er wird kommen;	becomes in subjunctive	er <u>werde</u> kommen
PERFECT	er hat gemacht;	" " "	er <u>habe</u> gemacht
	or ist gekommen;	" " "	er <u>sei</u> gekommen
PLUPERFECT	er hatte gemacht;	" " "	er <u>hätte</u> gemacht
	er war gekommen;	" " "	er <u>wäre</u> gekommen

VOCABULARY I

die Bus̲s̲e	penance, repentance
Bus̲s̲e tun	to do penance, repent
das Gelüst(e)	lust
die Gemeinde(n)	congregation, local church, community
geschehen (insep.)	to happen, come to pass
hassen	to hate
heiligen	to hallow, sanctify
ja	yes, indeed
-mal (note <u>c</u>)	time(s)
der Mörder(-)	murderer
nein	no
nun	now
das Ohr(en)	ear
reuen	to regret, rue
es reut mich (note <u>d</u>)	I regret it
selber (=selbst; see Lesson VII, note <u>e</u>)	
senden (p.p. <u>gesandt</u>)	to send
die Sprache(n)	language, speech
suchen	to seek, look for, attempt
sündigen	to sin
der Teufel(-)	devil
töten	to kill
unehelich	out of wedlock
vergeben (insep.) (+<u>dat.</u>)	to forgive
warum	why
wider (+<u>acc.</u>)	against
wieder	again
wieder/kommen (sep.) (imp. <u>kam</u>)	to come back, return

SENTENCES

1. Und Gott sprach: 'Es werde Licht!' Und es wurde Licht. (Gn. 1:3)

2. Er aber sagte zu ihnen: 'Wenn ihr betet, sagt: Unser Vater im Himmel, dein Name werde geheiligt (note <u>a</u>). Dein Reich komme. Dein Wille geschehe, wie im Himmel, so auch auf Erden' (note <u>b</u>). (Lk. 11:2)

3. Wer ein Ohr hat, der höre, was der Geist den Gemeinden sagt. (Rev. 2:7, etc.)

4. Wer sagt, er sei im Licht, und seinen Bruder hass̲t, der ist noch in der Finsternis. (1 Jn. 2:9)

5. Er aber sagte: 'Nein, Vater Abraham, sondern wenn einer von den Toten zu ihnen ginge, so würden sie Busse tun.' (Lk. 16:30)

6. Wenn dein Bruder siebenmal (note c) wider dich sündigen würde und siebenmal zu dir wiederkäme und sagte: 'Es reut mich' (note d), so sollst du ihm vergeben. (Lk. 17:4)

7. Sie antworteten und sagten zu ihm: 'Abraham ist unser Vater.' Jesus sagte zu ihnen: 'Wenn ihr Abrahams Kinder wäret, so tätet ihr Abrahams Werke. Nun aber sucht ihr mich zu töten, einen Menschen, der ich euch die Wahrheit gesagt habe (note e), die ich von Gott gehört habe. Das hat Abraham nicht getan. Ihr tut die Werke eures Vaters.' Da sagten sie zu ihm: 'Wir sind nicht unehelich geboren; wir haben e i n e n Vater: Gott.' Jesus sagte zu ihnen: 'Wäre Gott euer Vater (note f), so würdet ihr mich lieben, denn ich bin ausgegangen und komme von Gott; denn ich bin nicht von mir selber gekommen, sondern Er hat mich gesandt. Warum kennt ihr denn meine Sprache nicht? (note g). Denn ihr könnt mein Wort nicht hören. Ihr seid von dem Vater, dem Teufel, und die Gelüste eures Vaters wollt ihr tun. Der ist ein Mörder von Anfang.' (Jn. 8:39-44)

8. Sie sind von uns ausgegangen, aber sie waren nicht von uns, denn wenn sie von uns gewesen wären, so wären sie ja bei uns geblieben. (note h) (1 Jn. 2:19)

GRAMMATICAL NOTES

a. Dein Name werde geheiligt ('Thy name be hallowed')

Mein Sohn ... ist gefunden worden ('My son ... has been found'.)

The passive voice is formed with werden and the past participle. In the perfect (and pluperfect) passive, geworden becomes worden.

b. auf Erden

The -n is an old case-ending which has survived in this fixed phrase.

c. siebenmal

-mal can be added to any number in the sense of 'time(s)', e.g. einmal, 'once'; zweimal, 'twice'; siebzigmal sieben, 'seventy times seven'.

d. Es reut mich

This cannot be translated literally into modern English, but cf. AV English: 'it repenteth me' (Gn. 6:7). Such 'impersonal' constructions (i.e. where es does not refer to any particular noun) are common in German. (Cf. Es werde Licht.)

e. Ihr sucht mich ..., der ich ... die Wahrheit gesagt habe

This construction occurs in relative clauses when the antecedent (here: mich) is 1st or 2nd person, singular or plural. It enables the verb in the relative clause to have a 1st or 2nd person subject, which it otherwise would not have. Cf. one form of the Lord's Prayer: 'Vater unser, der du bist im Himmel ...' (Here the antecedent - Vater unser - is vocative, therefore in effect 2nd person singular).

f. Wäre Gott euer Vater ...

For this construction, see Lesson V, note d.

g. Warum kennt ihr denn meine Sprache nicht?

Denn is not only a conjunction ('for'), but is used as a 'particle' inside a clause in the sense of 'then': 'Why then do ye not know my speech?'

h. So wären sie ja bei uns geblieben

Ja (normal meaning 'yes') is often used as an unstressed particle to add emphasis or certainty to a statement. Frequently untranslatable. Cf. Lesson XV, note e.

j. zu Laodicea ('at L.'); zum Gericht ('for the purpose of judgment');

zu den Füssen des Engels ('at the feet of the angel').

Notice the wide range of meanings covered by the preposition zu. The first two occur frequently; the third is an idiom.

k. der, welcher mit dir redet ('he who is talking with thee')

When the antecedent is an emphatic pronoun (der, etc.) a relative pronoun in the same case is usually welcher (etc.), in order to avoid the awkward combination 'der, der ...'.

l. ich bin ... Mitknecht ... derer, die ... ('I am the fellowservant ...

of those who ...

Derer is gen. of the emphatic pronoun die (plural). It is also occasionally found as a relative pronoun. Cf. Lesson XV, note m. iii.

m. der sei weiter böse ('let him continue to be wicked')

Weiter is often used with verbs in the above sense.

VOCABULARY II

ach!	oh!
an/beten (sep.)	to worship
aus/speien (sep.)	to spit out
bald	soon
böse	evil, wicked, angry
da (conjunction)	as, since
damit (conjunction)	in order that
einige (plural)	some, a few
der Engel(-)	angel
finden (imp. fand; p.p. gefunden)	to find
fromm	godly, pious
ganz	(adj.) whole, (adv.) quite, altogether
geboren	born
das Gericht(e)	judgment, law-court
(hin)aus/stossen (sep.) (imp. stiess; p.p. gestossen)	to thrust out, expel
kalt	cold
lau	lukewarm, tepid
lehren	to teach
der (Mit)knecht(e)	(fellow)servant
nah(e)	near
nichts	nothing

nieder/fallen (sep.)	to fall down
(imp. **fiel**)	
die Schöpfung	creation
selig	blessed, overjoyed, in heaven, deceased, late
treu	faithful
(un)rein	(im)pure
verlieren (insep.)	to lose
(p.p. verlóren)	
versiegeln (insep.)	to seal up
wahr	true
wahrháftig	truthful
weder ... noch	neither ... nor
weil	because
die Weissagung(en)	prophecy
weit	far, distant
weiter (comparative of above) (note **m**)	further
welcher (like **def**. article) (note **k**)	which
die Zeit(en)	time
zú/sehen (sep.)	to watch, take heed
(pres. **sieht**)	
zuverlässig	reliable

FURTHER EXAMPLES

9. Denn dieser mein Sohn war tot und ist wieder lebéndig geworden; er war verlóren und ist gefunden worden. (note **a**) (Lk. 15:24)

10. Und dem Engel der Geméinde zu Laodicea (note **j**) schreibe: 'Das sagt Amen, der treue und wahrháftige Zeuge, der Anfang der Schöpfung Gottes: Ich <u>weiss</u> deine Werke, <u>dass</u> du weder kalt noch warm bist. Ach, <u>dass</u> du kalt oder warm wärest! Weil du aber lau bist, und weder kalt noch warm, werde ich dich aus meinem Munde áusspeien.' (Rev. 3:14-16)

11. Der Mensch antwortete und sagte zu ihnen: 'Wäre dieser nicht von Gott, so könnte er nichts tun.' Sie antworteten und sagten zu ihm: 'Du bist ganz in Sünden geboren, und lehrst du uns?' Und sie stiessen ihn hináus. Jesus hörte, <u>dass</u> sie ihn áusgestossen hatten, und als er ihn fand, sagte er zu ihm: 'Glaubst du an den Sohn Gottes?' Er antwortete und sagte: 'Herr, wer ist es? <u>dass</u> ich an ihn glaube.' Jesus sagte zu ihm: 'Du hast ihn gesehen, und der, welcher (note **k**) mit dir redet, der ist es.' Er aber sagte: 'Herr, ich glaube!' und betete ihn an. Und Jesus sagte: 'Ich bin zum Gericht (note **j**) in diese Welt gekommen, damít die, welche nicht sehen, sehend werden, und die, welche sehen, blind werden.' Das hörten einige der Pharisäer, die bei ihm waren, und sie sagten zu ihm: 'Sind wir denn auch blind?' Jesus sagte zu ihnen: 'Wäret ihr blind, so hättet ihr keine Sünde; da ihr aber sagt: "Wir sind sehend", so bleibt eure Sünde.' (Jn. 9:30,33-41)

12. Und er sagte zu mir: 'Diese Worte sind zuvérlässig und wahr, und der Herr, der Gott der Geister der Propheten, hat seinen Engel gesandt, um seinen Knechten zu zeigen, was bald geschehen <u>muss</u>. Siehe, ich komme bald. Selig ist der, welcher die Worte der Weissagung in diesem Buch hält.' Und ich bin Johánnes, der dies gesehen und gehört hat. Und als ich es gehört und gesehen hatte, fiel ich nieder, um zu den

Füssen (note j) des Engels ánzubeten, der mir dies zeigte. Und er sagte zu mir: 'Siehe zu, tu es nicht; denn ich bin dein Mitknecht und
deiner Brüder, der Prophéten, und derer, die (note l) die Worte dieses
Buches halten; bete Gott an.' Und er sagte zu mir: 'Versíegle nicht
die Worte dieser Weissagung in diesem Buch, denn die Zeit ist nahe.
Wer böse ist, der sei weiter (note m) böse; und wer únrein ist, der
sei weiter únrein; aber wer fromm ist, der sei weiter fromm, und wer
heilig ist, der sei weiter heilig.' (Rev. 22:6-11)

Lesson XI

In this and subsequent lessons, no grammatical introduction will be
given, though the grammatical notes between the reading passages will continue as before. In the vocabularies, where an entry is related to other
important biblical or theological words, these are given too. See also the
composite vocabulary at the end of the course.

VOCABULARY I

áuf/erstehen (sep.) (p.p. erstand)	to rise (from the dead)
die Áuferstehung	resurrection
bedéuten (insep.)	to mean, to signify
die Bedéutung(en)	meaning
éin/setzen (sep.)	to appoint, install
erfüllen (insep.)	to fulfil
die Erfüllung	fulfilment
errétten (insep.)	to save, deliver
der Errétter(-)	saviour, deliverer
die Erréttung	salvation, deliverance
erwécken (insep.)	to awaken, rouse
die Erwéckung(en)	revival, awakening
der Fluch(ü/e)	curse
(verflúcht	accursed)
herrschen (cf. Herr)	to rule, hold sway, prevail
der Herrscher(-)	ruler, sovereign
Jesája	Isaiah
das Kapítel(-)	chapter
das Kreuz(e)	cross
kreuzigen	to crucify
die Kreuzigung	crucifixion
die Macht(ä/e)	power, might
(die Allmacht	omnipotence)

(all)mächtig	(al)mighty
(der Allmächtige	the Almighty)
die Sünde(n)	sin
der Sünder(-)	sinner
sündhaft	sinful
sündigen	to sin
sündlos	sinless
tragen (pres. trägt)	to carry, bear, wear
überwinden (insep.)	to overcome
die Überwindung	overcoming
verlassen (insep.)	to leave, abandon
die Verlassenheit	abandoned state, dereliction
zugleich	at the same time

FIRST PASSAGE

Christi Sterben (note a) bedeutet, dass der Sündlose unter dem Fluch in die Gottverlassenheit (note b) der 'polloi' (Jes. 53,11) (Jesaja, Kapitel dreiundfünfzig, Vers elf) geht. Die Überwindung des Fluches ist er aber als der Auferstandene (note c). Als der Auferstandene ist er in die Herrschermacht (note b) eingesetzt ... der kommende Weltrichter ist zugleich der Erretter; weil Gott die Erweckung aus den Toten in ihm erfüllte; er trägt den Menschennamen (note b) Jesu, den Namen des Gekreuzigten (note c).

> (Schniewind, 'Die Leugner der Auferstehung in Korinth',
> in Nachgelassene Reden und Aufsätze, Berlin, 1952.)

GRAMMATICAL NOTES

a. Christi Sterben (literally: 'Christ's dying')

> Most infinitives can be turned into gerunds (verbal nouns) by the use of an initial capital letter. Such nouns are neuter, and unless preceded by a genitive (as above), or in fixed phrases, will generally be found with the article, e.g.: das Schreiben, 'writing'; das Sprechen, 'speaking'; das Wiedersehen, 'seeing again', 'meeting' (cf. auf Wiedersehen, 'goodbye').

b. Gottverlassenheit; Herrschermacht ('sovereign power'); Menschennamen ('human name')

> i. One of the most obvious features of German is its tendency to use lengthy compound words. The only way to master these is to break them down into their component parts, ascertain the meaning of the parts, and then reassemble the whole. The larger German-English dictionaries are often helpful on compounds (usually treated as subsidiary entries below the keyword), though the almost limitless range of possibilities proves too much at times even for the most comprehensive dictionary. The gender and plural of a compound noun are always those of the last element; thus the first two nouns given above are feminine; the third is masculine.

> ii. Gottverlassenheit is also worthy of comment as an example of an abstract noun ending in -heit. Most nouns with this suffix are abstract, and all are feminine. The force of -heit can sometimes be compared with that of English '-ness'; literally, therefore, the noun above means 'God-abandonedness'. Further examples:

Kleinheit, 'smallness'; Bosheit, 'malice, spite'; Lauheit, 'luke-warmness'; Reinheit, 'purity'.

c. der Auferstandene ('the Risen One'); des Gekreuzigten ('of the Cruci-fied')

Just as ordinary adjectives can be used as nouns (e.g. der Erste, Lesson IV, note c), so can participles used adjectivally (e.g. present participle: den Sehenden, Lesson IX, note f; past partici-ples: above).

d. ihres Gott-Nicht-Erkennens ('of their not knowing God')

i. Another example of a compound noun, hyphenated because consciously formed from a word-cluster within a clause, i.e. '(dass sie) Gott nicht erkennen'. The infinitive (erkennen) is here used as a neuter noun, hence the capital letter and the final genitive s. Other examples of this common usage are found in this passage: das Eingehen auf = entering into; Erkanntsein = being known; des Mitsterbens = of dying together.

ii. The first sentence of this passage provides a good example of the difference between wissen and (er)kennen, first touched on in Lesson V, note a. Translate: 'What the heathen know about God is only an aspect of their failure truly to know God.'

e. Gott liess seine 'Doxa' aufleuchten ('God caused His glory to shine forth')

Lassen plus an infinitive is an important German construction. The infinitive accompanying lassen is always active in form, though in English it sometimes needs a passive to translate it, e.g.:
er liess ihn seinen Vater rufen, 'he got him (caused him) to call his father' (active);
er liess ihn rufen, 'he had him called' (= caused him to be called) (passive).

With a reflexive pronoun, the above construction tends to mean 'to allow (itself) to be done', e.g.:
er liess sich nicht erkennen, 'he did not allow himself to be recog-nized';
das Wasser lässt sich nicht trinken, 'the water does not allow itself to be drunk', i.e. is undrinkable.

f. nichts anderes als ('nothing other than')

i. After nichts ('nothing') and etwas ('something') the adjective adds the neuter ending -es, which may decline, e.g. mit nichts anderem (dat.). Many adjectives also acquire a capital letter in this construction, becoming in effect neuter adjectival nouns, e.g. nichts Neues, 'nothing new'; etwas Grosses, 'something big'.

ii. N.B. als also means 'than' after comparatives, e.g. er ist grösser als ich, 'he is bigger than I'.

g. das immer schon geschehene Erkanntsein (literally: '(the state of) being known which has always occurred already', i.e. 'which is invariably found to be a pre-existing fact'); in den das gesamte

<u>Leben eröffnenden Ruf Gottes</u> ('into the call of God which opens up
the entire life')

A marked feature of German literary style is the 'compound adjective',
which is a 'shorthand' method of expressing what would otherwise be a
relative clause. In order to arrive at the meaning, therefore, the
reader should mentally expand the phrase, into the relative clause,
and translate (or paraphrase!) accordingly. The two examples above
would be expanded thus:
das Erkanntsein, das immer schon geschehen ist;
in den Ruf Gottes, der das gesamte Leben eröffnet.
(Traces of the 'shorthand' method are found also in English, e.g.
'all-embracing reality'='reality which embraces all'.)

<u>h</u>. <u>Erkanntsein durch</u> Gott ('(a state of) being known by God')

   i. In Lesson X (note <u>a</u>) it was stated that the German <u>passive</u> voice
   is formed from <u>werden</u> plus past participle. However, if a <u>state
   of affairs</u> is being described, rather than an action, the construction is <u>sein</u> plus past participle. The following two examples will
   make the distinction clear:

   Das Buch wird geschrieben, 'the book is being written'.
   Das Buch ist schon geschrieben, 'the book <u>is</u> already written'.

   ii. The <u>agent</u> of a passive verb is introduced by <u>von</u> (+<u>dat</u>.), e.g.
   Das Buch wird <u>von</u> einem Theologen geschrieben.
   The <u>instrument</u> of a passive verb is introduced by <u>durch</u> (+<u>acc</u>.)
   e.g.: Wir werden <u>durch</u> den Glauben gerechtfertigt, 'We are justi-
   fied by faith'.

   However in the phrase under discussion, Erkanntsein <u>von</u> Gott would
   have been ambiguous (because <u>von</u> may mean 'of'), i.e. the phrase could
   mean '<u>God's</u> state of being known'. In such cases, therefore, <u>durch</u>
   (+<u>acc</u>.) replaces <u>von</u>.

<u>j</u>. <u>eine immer intensivere</u> Erfahrung ('an ever more intensive experience')

   <u>Immer</u> plus <u>comparative</u> is used in such expressions as the following:
   immer <u>grösser</u>, 'bigger and bigger'; <u>immer mehr</u>, 'more and more'.

<u>k</u>. <u>des Mitsterbens mit ihm</u> ('of dying together with Him')

   <u>Mitsterben</u> (sep.) = 'to die with (someone)', 'to experience a common
   death'. Cf. <u>Mitknecht</u> 'fellow-servant' (Lesson X).

<u>VOCABULARY II</u>

ander (als)	other (than)
auf/leuchten (sep.)	to flash forth, beam out
eingehen (sep.) auf (or in)	to enter into
(+<u>acc</u>.)	
das Ende(n)	end
enden	to end
sich ereignen (insep.)	to occur
das Ereignis(se)	event, occurrence
erfahren (insep.)	to experience
die Erfahrung(en)	experience

erkénnen (insep.) (p.p. **erkánnt**)	to recognize, know personally
die Erkénntnis (Gótteserkenntnis	recognition, personal knowledge knowledge of God)
eröffnen (insep.)	to open, open up
gesámt	total, whole, entire
der Heide(n)	heathen, pagan
heidnisch	heathen, pagan (adj.)
immer	always, ever
jédoch	however
lassen (imp. liess) (+ infinitive)	to let; to leave; to cause (note e)
nie (or niemals)	never
noch einmal	once more
nur	only
der Ruf(e)	call, calling, reputation
schon	already
die Sprache(n)	language
zur Sprache kommen	to be put into words, to be talked about, discussed
verbínden (insep.) (p.p. verbúnden)	to link, connect
die Verbíndung(en)	connection
die Weise(n)	way, manner, aspect
weise	wise
die Weisheit	wisdom
die Wéisheitsliteratur	wisdom literature
die Wéisheitsrede	wisdom utterances
das Wissen um(+acc.)	knowledge of, about

SECOND PASSAGE

Das Wissen der Heiden um Gott ist nur eine Weise .ihres Gott-Nicht-Erkénnens (note d). In Christus liess jédoch Gott noch einmal seine 'Doxa' áufleuchten (note c) (2 Kor. 4,6)(zweiter Koríntherbrief, Kapítel vier, Vers sechs). Das Wort dieser Doxa ist das Wort des Evangéliums und der Wéisheitsrede der Apostel und Prophéten. Gótteserkenntnis ist nichts anderes (note f) als das Eíngehen auf das immer schon geschehene (note g) Erkánntsein durch Gott (note h), das im Evangélium zur Sprache kam und für mich Eréignis wurde (Röm. 8,29 f.)(Römerbrief, Kapítel acht, Vers neunundzwanzig und folgende). Sie ist mit der Liebe verbúnden (1 Kor. 8,1 ff.; 13,2)(erster Koríntherbrief, Kapítel acht, Vers eins und folgende; Kapítel dreizehn, Vers zwei) und bedéutet ein nie endendes existentiélles Eíngehen in den das gesámte Leben eröffnenden Ruf Gottes (note g) in Jesus Christus (Eph. 3, 16-19) (Ephéserbrief, Kapítel drei, Vers sechzehn bis neunzehn) und eine immer intensívere (note j) Erfáhrung des Mitsterbens (note k) mit ihm (Phil. 3, 8-14)(Philípperbrief, Kapítel drei, Vers acht bis vierzehn).

  (Synopsis of Heinrich Schlier, 'Die Erkénntnis Gottes nach den Paulusbriefen', a contribution to Gott in Welt: Festgabe für Karl Rahner, I, 1964; synopsis given in Internationale Zeitschriftenschau für Bibelwissenschaft und Grenzgebiete, Band XI, 1964-5, S.177, Patmos-Verlag, Düsseldorf.)

Lesson XII

VOCABULARY I

sich án/schliessen (sep.)(+<u>dat</u>.)	to attach oneself, to associate
(p.p. <u>geschlossen</u>)	oneself with
beéinflussen (insep.)	to influence
(der Éinfluss auf +<u>acc</u>.	influence on)
bekánntlich (cf. kennen)	as is well known
bewáhren (insep.) vor (+<u>dat</u>.)	to keep, preserve from
bishér	hitherto
dámit	thereby
entfállen (insep.) auf	to fall to
(+<u>acc</u>.)	someone's share
	be apportioned to
entschéiden (insep.)	to decide, be decisive
die Entschéidung(en)	decision, decree
das Erbe	inheritance
erben	to inherit
die Erbsünde	original sin
erhében (insep.)	to raise
(p.p. erhóben)	
erklären (insep.)	to explain, declare
fällen	to pass (law, etc.)
fest	firm(ly)
das Gebíet(e)	district, region, field (of
	activity, thought, etc.)
das Gesicht(er)	face
der Gesíchtspunkt(e)	point of view, viewpoint
die Glaubenslehre (cf. Glaube,	doctrine, dogma, doctrinal
Lehre)	system
gläubig	believing
der Gläubige(n)	believer
die Gruppe(n)	group
das Heil	salvation
der Heiland	Saviour
die Heilsgeschichte	history of salvation
heilsnotwendig (note <u>d</u>)	necessary for salvation
die Himmelfahrt	ascension to heaven
(leibliche Himmelfahrt	bodily assumption)
isolíeren (note <u>j</u>)	to isolate
das Jahrhúndert(e)(cf. Jahr,	century
hundert)	
das Léhramt(ä/er)(cf. lehren)	magisterium, teaching office
léhramtlich	of the magisterium
(das Amt	office)
die Meinung(en)	opinion, view
die Neuzeit (cf. neu, Zeit)	recent times
ökuménisch	ecumenical
die ökuménische Bewégung	the ecumenical movement

der Papst(ä/e)	pope
päpstlich	papal
römisch (cf. Rom)	Roman
römisch-katholisch	Roman-Catholic
schliessen	to close, shut
schliesslich	final(ly)
standhaft	steadfast
stark	strong(ly)
unterscheiden (insep.)	to differentiate
die Unterscheidung	differentiation
der Unterschied(e)	difference
verändern (insep.)(cf. ander)	change
die Veränderung(en)	alteration, change
verschieden	different, various
vertréten (insep.)	to represent, advocate, uphold
(p.p. vertréten)	(opinion, etc.)
voneinánder	from one another
das Vórgehen	progress, action, procedure
während (conjunction)	while
(preposition)(+gen.)	during
wéiter/entwickeln (sep.)	to develop further
(die Entwicklung(en)	development)
wichtig	important
zum Beispiel (z.B.)	for example
zwischen (+acc. or dat.)	between

FIRST PASSAGE

Bekánntlich ist kein Gebíet der kathólischen Dogmátik in der Neuzeit so
stark (note a) wéiterentwickelt worden wie die Lehre von María, der Mutter
Jesu. Von den drei grossen léhramtlichen Entschéidungen, die im 19.
(neunzehnten) und bisher im 20. (zwanzigsten) Jahrhúndert gefállt worden
sind, entfállen zwei auf die Mariologie. 1854 (áchtzehnhundertvierund-
fünfzig)(note b) erklärte Papst Pius IX (der Neunte) die Meinung, dass die
Mutter Jesu vor der Erbsünde bewáhrt worden sei, (note c) müsse héilsnot-
wendigerweise (note d) von allen Gläubigen fest und standhaft (note a) ver-
tréten werden (note c). Im Jahr 1950 (neunzehnhundertfunfzig)(note b) hat
schliesslich Papst Pius XII (der Zwölfte) die leibliche Himmelfahrt Maríens
(note e) zu einem Dogma erhóben. Damit ist die Mariologie zu einer der
wichtigsten Unterschéidungslehren zwischen den christlichen Kirchen geworden (note f). Denn weder der Protestantismus (note g) noch die Orthodoxie
haben sich bisher diesen römischen Entschéidungen ángeschlossen. In unserer
klein gewordenen Welt (note h) können die christlichen Konfessiónen aber
nicht mehr isoliert (note j) voneinánder leben. Die Glaubenslehre der ver-
schíedenen Gruppen muss zwischen ihnen zur Sprache kommen und auch das
weitere Vórgehen beeínflussen. So hat z.B. während des Zweiten Vatikáni-
schen Konzíls die mariológische Diskussión durch ökuménische Gesíchtspunkte
Veränderungen erfáhren.

(Prof. Dr. Gerhard Müller, 'Pius IX und die Entwicklung der römisch-
katholischen Mariologie.' Inaugural lecture at Érlangen, 18 Jan. 1968.
In Neue Zeitschrift für systemátische Theologie, herausg. C.H. Ratschow.
10. Band, 1968, Heft 2, S.111.)

GRAMMATICAL NOTES

<u>a</u>. stark ('strongly'); <u>fest und standhaft</u> ('firmly and steadfastly')

The German <u>adverb</u> is normally the same in form as the uninflected <u>adjective</u> and remains invariable at all times. See, however, note <u>d</u> below.

<u>b</u>. <u>1854</u> (achtzehnhundertvierundfünfzig); im Jahr 1950 (neunzehnhundertfünfzig)

i. numbers written out in full usually appear as one word.

ii. 'in' a certain year is either omitted altogether, or expressed by im Jahr(e)

<u>c</u>. dass die Mutter ... <u>bewahrt worden sei</u> ('that the Mother ... had been preserved ...');

die Meinung ... <u>müsse ... vertreten werden</u> ('the view must be upheld')

Here are two typical examples of a verb-cluster at the end of a clause. A useful method of 'disentangling' them is as follows:

i. Rearrange verbs, if necessary, so that the <u>active verb</u> stands <u>first</u> in the group, e.g.:

$$1 \qquad 2 \qquad 3 \qquad 1 \qquad 2 \qquad 3$$

<u>sei</u> bewahrt worden;   <u>müsse</u> vertreten werden

ii. Start with the first verb; jump to the last verb; then work back, e.g.:

$$1 \qquad 3 \qquad 2 \qquad 1 \qquad 3 \qquad 2$$

sei worden bewahrt;   müsse werden vertreten

'had' 'been' 'preserved';   'must' 'be' 'upheld'

likewise if a group of <u>four</u> verbs occurs, read them in the order:

$$1, 4, 3, 2.$$

<u>d</u>. héilsnotwendigerweise ('as necessary for salvation')

i. nótwendig = 'necessary'

ii. a few adjectives may sometimes be found with the suffix <u>-erweise</u>, which turns them into adverbs. Here are some common examples:

möglicherweise	'possibly'
erstaunlicherweise	'surprisingly'
dummerweise	'stupidly'
glücklicherweise	'fortunately'

<u>e</u>. Himmelfahrt Mariéns

Notice this rather exceptional <u>gen</u>. When <u>María</u> occurs in compounds, it appears as <u>Marién-</u>, e.g. die Mariénkirche, 'St. Mary's Church'; das Mariénbild, 'image of the Virgin Mary'.

<u>f</u>. die Mariologíe ist <u>zu</u> ... geworden

i. The vast majority of borrowed words ending in <u>-ie</u> are stressed on _n._ <u>War doch</u> vom Konzil ... Maria ... geziert worden ('Mary had, <u>after all</u>, been adorned ... by the Council ...')

This special use of <u>doch</u>, after a verb (or verb plus subject), should be noted.

_o._ <u>Gottesgebärerin</u>

Note the fem. suffix -<u>in</u>, and its use in such examples as:

| Königin | 'queen' | Christin | 'Christian woman' |
| Lehrerin | 'lady teacher' | Jüdin | 'Jewess' |

_p._ Deswegen <u>wurde</u> ... von einer unbefleckten Empfängnis ... <u>gesprochen</u>. ('<u>Thus ... an immaculate conception ... was talked about</u>')

i. The sentence might have read as follows:
Es <u>wurde</u> deswegen ... von einer unbefleckten Empfängnis <u>gesprochen</u>. In this passive construction, <u>es</u> is used impersonally, i.e. without reference to any neuter noun. Such constructions have to be paraphrased in English, rather than translated. Further examples:

<u>es</u> wird gesungen, 'there is singing';
<u>es</u> wurde diskutiert, 'there was discussion'.

ii. If inversion of subject and verb occurs for any reason, this impersonal <u>es</u> drops out (see sentence above); further examples:

In der Kirche wird gesungen; Wann wurde diskutiert?

_q._ <u>von Adam her</u> ('from Adam')

The addition of <u>her</u> avoids ambiguity, since 'der Makel der <u>von Adam</u> ererbten Schuld' could mean 'the taint of the guilt inherited <u>by</u> Adam' (for <u>von</u> with the passive, see Lesson XI, note _h_. ii). <u>Her</u> is frequently used to express the idea of 'from' some place of origin (or 'towards the speaker'), e.g.:

woher, whence; er kam her<u>aus</u>, 'he came out'; er kam her<u>über</u>, 'he came across'.

Its opposite is <u>hin</u>, denoting 'to' some destination (or 'away from the speaker'), e.g.:

wohin, 'whither'; dorthin, 'thither'; er ging hin<u>aus</u>, 'he went out'; er ging hin<u>über</u>, 'he went across'.

VOCABULARY II

ab	(see <u>von</u> ... <u>ab</u>)
an/sehen (sep.)	to look at
ansehen <u>als</u>	to regard as
befreien (insep.)(cf. frei)	to free
die Christenheit	Christendom
deswegen	thus, therefore, for that reason
doch (note <u>n</u>)	yet, nonetheless, after all
dringen	to urge
dringend	urgent
empfangen (insep.)	to receive; conceive (child)
die Empfängnis	conception
(die unbefleckte Empfängnis	immaculate conception)

this ending; all are feminine, e.g. die Orthodox_ie_; die Philo-
soph_ie_; die Theolog_ie_.

ii. Particularly in literary style, <u>werden</u> in its sense of 'to become'
frequently has <u>zu</u> + <u>dat</u>. where English would have an ordinary
complement, i.e. this <u>zu</u> should not be translated.

g. <u>der Protestantismus</u>

The suffix -<u>ismus</u> is the usual equivalent of English -ism. Here are
some common examples, with related words:

(MOVEMENT)	(ADJECTIVE)	(ADHERENT)
der Protestantismus	protestántisch	der Protestánt(en)
der Katholizismus	kathólisch	der Katholik(en)
der Mystizismus	mýstisch	der Mýstiker(-)
der Kommunismus	kommunistisch	der Kommunist(en)
der Atheismus	atheistisch	der Atheist(en)
der Existentialismus	existentialistisch	der Existentialist (en)
der Rationalismus	rationalistisch	der Rationalist(en)

h. <u>in unserer klein gewordenen Welt</u> = 'in our world which has become (so)
small' (see Lesson XI, note <u>g</u>).

j. <u>isoliert</u> (p.p. of <u>isolieren</u>)

There are scores of borrowed verbs ending in -ieren. All are weak, but
form their past participles without ge-. (In this respect they are like
inseparable verbs, see Lesson IX, note <u>b</u>.) Some further examples:

studieren (p.p. studiert)	'to study'
existieren (p.p. existiert)	'to exist'
entmythologisieren (p.p. entmythologisiert)	'to demythologize'
philosophieren (p.p. philosophiert)	'to philosophize'
telefonieren (p.p. telefoniert)	'to telephone'

k. <u>erst</u> im Mittelalter ('<u>not until</u> the Middle Ages')

<u>erst</u> is commonly used as an adverb with expressions of time; further
examples:
<u>erst</u> jetzt, '<u>only</u> now'; <u>erst</u> im zwanzigsten Jahrhundert, '<u>not until</u> the
20th century'.

l. <u>und zwar</u> in der westlichen Christenheit ('in Western Christendom, to be
precise')

After a <u>general</u> phrase, <u>und zwar</u> introduces a more <u>specific</u> one; e.g. im
Jahre 1970, <u>und zwar</u> im September, 'in 1970, September in fact'.

m. empfand <u>man</u> es als dringend ... ('it was felt to be urgent ...')

This very important pronoun corresponds closely to French 'on', being
used 'vaguely', i.e. without reference to any specific person(s). Its
English translation will depend entirely on what sounds best in each
case (see the tentative suggestions in Vocabulary II). However, a
<u>passive</u> construction is often the most natural one in English (see
translation above). <u>Man</u> invariably takes a 3rd person singular verb.

die Empfängnisverhütung	contraception
empfínden (insep.)	to feel, be sensible of
(imp. empfánd)	
erérbt (cf. erben)	hereditary, inherited
erst (adv.)(note k)	not until, only (with time expressions)
gebären (insep.)	to bear (child)
(p.p. gebóren)	
(die Góttesgebärerin (note o)	'God-bearer', Mother of God)
gleich	(adj.) same, equal; (adv.) immediately
(der/gleiche (both parts de-cline)	the same)
gléichzeitig (cf. Zeit)	at the same time
heissen	to be called, be stated, mean
das heisst (d.h.)	that is, i.e.
her	(note q)
konzipíeren	to conceive (idea)
der Makel(-)	taint, stain
man (note m)	one, 'you', 'they', people
misslich	dangerous, perilous
das Mittelalter	the Middle Ages
(das Alter(-)(cf. alt)	age)
(das Zeitalter	age, epoch, period)
die Schuld(en)	guilt, debt
schuldig	guilty
(únschuldig	innocent)
das Schúldopfer(-)	guilt-offering
sprechen (p.p. gesprochen)	to speak
der Titel(-)	title
(un)befléckt	(un)spotted, (un)stained
von ... ab	from ... onwards
von ... her (note q)	from
zeugen	to beget
(A zougto B	'A begat B')
die Zeugung	procreation, begetting
die Zierde(n)	adornment, ornament
zieren	to adorn
und zwar (note l)	'to be precise', in fact

SECOND PASSAGE

Die Immaculáta - Lehre ist erst im Mittelalter (note k), und zwar in der westlichen Christenheit (note l) konzipíert worden. Unter dem Einfluss der augustínischen Erbsündenlehre empfánd man (note m) es als dringend, die Mutter Jesu als von allen Makeln befréit zu sehen. War doch vom Konzil von Ephesus im Jahr 431 (vierhunderteinunddreissig) Maria mit dem Titel 'theotokos' ('Góttesgebärerin')(note o) geziert worden (note n). Es erschien misslich, sie gléichzeitig als unter dem Fluch der Erbsünde stehend ánzusehen. Deswegen wurde vom 12. (zwölften) Jahrhundert ab in der westlichen Christenheit von einer 'unbefleckten Empfängnis Mariens' gesprochen (note p). Das heisst, vom Moment ihrer Zeugung ab sei kein Makel an ihr gewesen, auch nicht der Makel der von Adam her (note q) ererbten Schuld.

(Prof. Dr. Gerhard Muller, op. cit.,
S. 112, 113.)

Lesson XIII

VOCABULARY I

	áb/tun (sep.)(p.p. getan)	to abolish
	án/nehmen (sep.)	to accept
	beschnéiden (insep.)	to circumcise
die	Beschnéidung	circumcision
	(schneiden	to cut)
	bestímmt	definite, certain, given
	betónen	to emphasize, stress
die	Betónung	emphasis, stress
	damals	at that time
	daraufhín	in view of this, so
	dürfen (pres. ich, er darf,	to be allowed to, 'may'
	du darfst)(note c)	
	eben	(adj.) even, level;
		(adv.) just, simply
	ebensowenig	just as little; likewise
		(in negative context)
	einfach	simple, simply
sich	ergében (insep.)	to result
	(pres. ergíbt	
	ergéhen (insep.)	to be issued (of laws, etc.)
	(p.p. ergángen)	
	fést/stellen (sep.)	to ascertain, establish
die	Frage(n)	question
	fragen	to ask
	gelten (pres. gilt)(+dat.)	to be valid for, apply to
	genúg	enough
	genügen	to suffice, be enough
	júdisch	Jewish
	legen	to lay, impose
	noch nicht (note d)	not yet
	ob	whether
	ohne (+acc.)	without
	ohne weiteres	without further ado
	prüfen	to check, examine
die	Prüfung(en)	examination
der	Sinn(e)	sense
	sinnlos	senseless
	sinnvoll	meaningful
	somít	thus, consequently
	übernéhmen (insep.)	to take over
	verbíeten (insep.)	to forbid, prohibit
	(p.p. verbóten)	
das	Verbót(e)	prohibition
der	Verstánd	intelligence
	verstéhen (insep.)	to understand
	(imp. verstánd; p.p. verstánden)	
	vieles	(more emphatic form of viel)
	wieweit	how far, to what extent

FIRST PASSAGE

Die christliche Kirche kann nicht ohne weiteres alle an Israel ergángenen Gebóte und Verbóte als auch ihr geltend annehmen. Jesus Christus ist 'des Gesétzes Ende' (Römerbrief 10,4) für seine Geméinde auch in dém Sinne (note a), dass vieles, das Israel (note b) als Gesétz gegeben war, für die Geméinde Jesu Christi ábgetan ist (Galáterbrief 4,10; Kolósserbrief 2,16f.). Paulus betónt, dass auf die Heiden, die zu Christus gekommen sind, nicht das jüdische Gesétz gelegt werden darf (note c). So hat die Christenheit zum Beispiel nie die Beschnéidung als Gebót Gottes für sich verstánden, ebensowenig das Sabbathgesetz. Sie kann das Israel gegebene Gesétz (note b) nicht in gesétzlichem Biblizísmus einfach übernéhmen, sondern sie muss ganz konkrét fragen, wiewéit und in welchem Sinne das Israel gegebene Gesétz auch ihr, der Kirche Christi gilt. Um mit Martin Luther zu sprechen: es genügt noch nicht féstzustellen (note d), dass ein bestímmtes Gebót damals Wort Gottes war, man muss auch fragen, ob es uns gesagt ist. Daraufhín muss das Gesétz und somít auch das zweite Gebót geprüft werden, im Lichte der Offenbárung Gottes, die in seinem Sohne Jesus Christus ergángen ist. So hat die Kirche es immer verstánden, wo sie die Freiheit durch Christus recht verstánd.

(continued in Second Passage below)

GRAMMATICAL NOTES

a. in dem Sinne, dass ... ('in this sense, that ...')

The unabbreviated form in dem (instead of im) serves to focus the reader's attention, in anticipation of the following dass - clause. The dem should therefore be stressed in reading, to indicate its intensified meaning. This emphatic use of the definite article has no precise parallel in English.

b. vieles, das Israel ... gegeben war; das Israel gegebene Gesetz

In both these phrases, Israel is in the dative case, being the indirect object of gegeben. With proper names, case must often be deduced solely from the context.

c. dass ... nicht das jüdische Gesetz gelegt werden darf ('that the Jewish law must not be imposed ...')

An important distinction is observed in German between the auxiliaries dürfen and müssen in negative sentences, e.g.:

    das jüdische Gesetz darf nicht ... gelegt werden, ' ... must not
                                                          be imposed'
    das jüdische Gesetz muss nicht... gelegt werden, ' ... does not have
                                                          to be imposed'

d. Um mit Martin Luther zu sprechen: es genügt noch nicht festzustellen ...
'To use Martin Luther's words: it is not enough merely to establish ...'

e. Bei solcher kritischen Prüfung im Lichte Jesu Christ ergibt sich ....
'The result of such a critical examination in the light of Jesus Christ is as follows ...'
Bei here has the sense of 'in the case of' (see Lesson XIV, note d).

<u>f</u>. Sollte Exodus 20,4 die Anfertigung von Bildern überhaupt ... gemeint
sein, so fiele das .... ('If in Exodus 20,4 the production of pictures
in general <u>were to</u> be meant, then this <u>would fall</u> ...')

    i. For inversion of subject and verb in sense of 'if ...', see
       Lesson V, note <u>d</u>.
   ii. For the use of the imperfect subjunctive in conditional sentences,
       see Lesson X.
  iii. Biblical references are often given without any introductory pre-
       position.

VOCABULARY II

án/fertigen (sep.)	to produce, make
die Anfertigung	production, manufacture
begründen (insep.)	to give reasons for, explain
sich begründen aus (+<u>dat</u>.)	to arise out of, be explained by
(der Grund(ü/e)	reason, ground, cause, bottom)
das Bild(er)	picture, image
binden	to bind, be binding on
dagégen	on the other hand
dár/stellen (sep.)	to represent, make a representation of
die Dárstellung(en)	presentation (of facts, etc.)
sich ergében (insep.)	to result
(pres. <u>ergíbt</u>)	
das Ergébnis(se)	result
fallen (imp. <u>fiel</u>; imp. subj. <u>fiele</u>)	to fall
der Gegenstand(ä/e)	object (i.e. 'thing'); subject (i.e. 'theme')
gegenständlich	in objective form
die Gegenwart	present (time), presence
gegenwärtig	present
die Gestált(en)	form, figure, shape
irdisch (cf. Erde)	earthly
meinen (cf. Meinung)	to mean, think, say
solch	such
überháupt	in general, at all
das Úrteil(e)	judgment, sentence
úrteilen	to judge, form a judgment
(verúrteilen (insep.)	to condemn)
(das Vór/urteil(e)	prejudice)
veréhren (insep.)	to revere, venerate
die Veréhrung	veneration
(die Ehre	honour)
das Wesen	essence, essential nature

SECOND PASSAGE (continued from First Passage, above)

    Bei solcher kritischen Prüfung im Lichte Jesu Christi ergíbt sich (note
<u>e</u>): sollte Exodus 20,4 die Anfertigung von Bildern überháupt und nicht nur
zur kultischen Veréhrung gemeint sein, so fiele das (note <u>f</u>) - wie Luther
geúrteilt hat - unter die Zeremoniálgebote, die nach Paulus durch das Kommen Christi ábgetan sind. Dagégen erkénnen wir in dem Verbót, Gott gégen-
ständlich in einem irdischen Bilde dárzustellen und dieses als Gestált
seiner Gégenwart kultisch zu veréhren, ein auch uns bindendes Gebót, weil

es aus dem Wesen und der Offenbárungsweise des Gottes Israels sich begründet, der auch unser Gott ist. Gott hat sich seine irdische Gestált durch
die Inkarnatión in Jesus Christus gegeben - in dem Sohne sollen wir ihn án-
beten, in keiner anderen Gestált.

(Paul Althaus, 'Die Illustratión der Bibel als theológisches Problem', in
<u>Neue Zeitschrift für systemátische Theologie</u>, 1. Band, Heft 2/3, 1959,
S. 317. Verlag Alfred Töpelmann, Berlin W 35.)

Lesson XIV

VOCABULARY I

absolvíeren	to complete (studies)
alléin	alone, only
der Bauer(n)(note <u>b</u>)	farmer, peasant
bäuerlich	peasant, rural
der Berg(e)	mountain
der Bergmann (pl. Bergleute)	miner
bestímmen (insep.) zu (+<u>dat</u>.)	to destine for
(die Vorhérbestimmung	fore-ordination, predestination)
bezíehen (insep.)(imp. <u>bezog</u>)	to enter (university, etc.)
dámalig (adj.)(cf. dámals)	of that time
dár/bringen (sep.)	to bring (a sacrifice, etc.)
deutsch	German (adj. and the German language)
der Deutsche(n) (<u>adj</u>. endings)	German (man)
Deutschland	Germany
éin/treten (sep.) in (+<u>acc</u>.)	to enter, go into
(imp. <u>trat</u>)	
die Eltern (pl. only)	parents
das Elternhaus (äu/er)	parental house, home
sich entschlíessen (insep.)	to make up one's mind
der Entschlúss(ü/e)	decision
der Eremít(en)(note <u>b</u>)	hermit, anchorite
erstícken (insep.)	to suffocate, stifle
die Fakultät(en)	faculty (of university)
fórt/setzen (sep.)	to continue (transitive)
fröhlich	cheerful, happy
die Frömmigkeit (cf. fromm)	piety
das (Ganz)opfer(-)(cf. ganz)	(whole) offering
gebóren (note <u>a</u>)	born

das Gemüt(er)	nature, disposition
gemütlich	cosy, snug, friendly, good-natured
genug	enough
gnädig (cf. Gnade)	gracious
hart	hard
die Jura (pl.)	law (academic discipline)
der Jurist(en)(note b)	lawyer
das Kloster(ö)	monastery, convent
der Knabe(n)(note b)	boy
die Kraft(ä/e)	power
kriegen	to get
das Lehrbuch(ü/er)	text-book
opfern	to sacrifice
der Opfertod	sacrificial death
die Partei(en)	party (religious, political, etc.)
plötzlich	sudden(ly)
die Scholastik	scholasticism
der Scholastiker	schoolman
statt (+gen., or zu +infin.)	instead of
das Studium(pl. Studien)	study, university course
üblich	usual, normal
unverwüstlich (cf. Wüste)	indestructible, imperturbable
vermögen (insep.) zu (+infin.)	to be able to
(imp. vermöchte)	
die Zucht	discipline
(Kirchenzucht	church discipline)
züchtigen	to discipline, chastise,
die Züchtigung	chastisement
zu/lassen (sep.)	to permit
(p.p. gelassen)	

FIRST PASSAGE

Die deutsche Reformation ist das Werk Martin Luthers, der am 10. (zehnten) November 1483 (vierzehnhundertdreiundachtzig) als Sohn eines Bergmanns aus bäuerlicher Familie geboren ist (note a). Die harte Zucht im frommen Elternhaus vermöchte die unverwüstliche Kraft eines fröhlichen Gemüts in dem Knaben (note b) nicht zu ersticken. Vom Vater zum Juristen (note b) bestimmt, bezog Luther im Jahre 1501 (fünfzehnhunderteins) die Universität Erfurt, an der unter den damaligen Parteirichtungen der Scholastik allein die Via moderna Ockams zugelassen war. Nach deren (note c) Lehrbücher absolvierte er das übliche Studium in der Artistenfakultät und wurde 1505 (fünfzehnhundertfünf) Magister ... Statt das Studium in der Juristenfakultät fortzusetzen, trat er am 17. (siebzehnten) Juli 1505 nach plötzlichem Entschluss in das Kloster der Augustinereremiten (note b) in Erfurt ein, um durch 'fromm werden und genug tun' ein 'Ganzopfer' darzubringen und 'einen gnädigen Gott' zu 'kriegen'.

(continued in Second Passage below)

GRAMMATICAL NOTES

a. der ... 1483 ... geboren ist ('who was born ...')

This use of the verb sein to form a passive is exceptional (see Lesson X, note a), as is also the present tense to indicate a past event. This particular phrase is commonly used of persons still living, e.g. ich bin

1940 geboren; in the case of persons no longer living, <u>ist</u> geboren can be replaced by (the more logical) <u>wurde</u> geboren.

<u>b</u>. in dem Kna<u>ben</u>; zum Juri<u>sten</u>; Kloster der Augusti<u>nereremiten</u>

These nouns belong to the comparatively large number of <u>masculines</u> denoting <u>living beings</u> which add -(e)n in all cases singular and plural except nom. singular. <u>Mensch</u> with its similar declension was mentioned in Lesson VII, note <u>b</u>. ii.

<u>c</u>. nach der<u>en</u> Lehrbücher ('according to its textbooks', i.e. the textbooks of Ockam's 'Via moderna')

    i. <u>deren</u> is the fem. gen. of the demonstrative pronoun <u>der</u> (cf. Lesson V, note <u>e</u>. ii). If the normal possessive adjective had been used (i.e. nach <u>ihren</u> Lehrbücher), it could theoretically have referred to any one of the previous fem. or plural nouns, e.g. Universität, Parteirichtungen, Scholastik, or Via moderna. <u>Deren</u>, however, restricts the reference to the last-named noun, so avoiding ambiguity.

    ii. For masc. or neut., <u>dessen</u> would be similarly used instead of <u>sein</u>, e.g.: er kam mit seinem Bruder und dessen Sohn, i.e. with the <u>brother's</u> son.

    iii. A complete table of relative demonstrative pronouns is given in Lesson XV, note <u>m</u>. i.

<u>d</u>. bei ihm ('in his case'); <u>bei</u> seinen Ordensbrüdern ('in (the case of) his brethren in the Order')

Note this possible meaning of <u>bei</u>. Another is 'in the works of' an author, e.g. diese Lehre finden wir <u>bei</u> Paulus.

<u>e</u>. wie er ... dem Begriff der Liebe entgegengesetzt ('as ... it <u>is</u> set over against the idea of love)

One would expect entgegengesetzt <u>ist</u>, but this auxiliary is omitted for economy of style, since <u>ist</u> occurs again at the end of the next clause: ... erfa<u>sst ist</u>. Cf. the omission of the auxiliary <u>hat</u> at the end of the first clause in the following: 'Jesus Christus, den der Vater geliebt und in die Welt gesandt hat ...'

<u>f</u>. mit seiner mystisch-evangelischen Frömmigkeit ('with his piety which combined mystical and evangelical elements')
Note the use of the hyphen in phrases of this kind. The first element remains undeclined. Cf. die römisch-katholische Kirche.

VOCABULARY II

ändern (cf. ander)	to change, alter
die Änderung(en)	change, alteration
aufmerksam auf (+acc.)	attentive to
die Aufmerksamkeit	attention, attentiveness
begreifen (insep.)	to comprehend, grasp
der Begriff(e)	idea, concept
bekennen (insep.)	to profess, confess
das Bekenntnis(se)	profession, confession(of faith)
die Bekenntniskirche(n)	confessional church

(das Glaubensbekenntnis	creed)
besónder(s)	especial(ly)
bríngen (imp. brachte)	to bring
die Démut	humility
démütig	humble, meek
entgégen/setzen (sep.)(+dat.)	to set over against
erfássen (insep.) als	to conceive as
erhóffen (insep.)	to hope for
(die Hoffnung(en)	hope)
ersáufen (insep.)	to drown (intrans.)
(p.p. ersóffen)	
erschrécken (insep.)	to frighten
fast	almost
fühlen	to feel
der Hínweis(e) auf(+acc.)	reference to
hín/weisen (sep.) auf(+acc.)	to refer to
insbesóndere (cf. besonder)	in particular
der Mönch(e)	monk
mönchisch(or Mönchs-)	monastic
der Orden(-)	order (monastic, etc.)
der Ordenstand	being in the order
sélbst/anklagend	self-accusing
(án/klagen (sep.)	to accuse)
sich steigern zu (+dat.)	to increase to
die Strafe(n)	punishment
strafen	to punish
die Tat(en)	deed, act
der Täter(-)	doer, culprit
tätig	active
die Tätigkeit(en)	activity
der Trost	comfort
trösten	to comfort
die Tugend(en)	virtue
tugendhaft	virtuous
der Umgang mit	association with
die (Un)ruhe	(dis)quiet
das Verständnis (cf. verstéhen)	understanding
verzwéifeln (insep.)	to despair
die Verzwéiflung	despair
vielméhr	rather
der Vórgesetzte(adj. endings)	superior, senior
wenig	little, not much
wenige (plural)	few
der Wert(e)	value, worth
die Willkür	arbitrariness
wíllkürlich	arbitrary, despotic
der Zústand(ä/e)	condition, state

SECOND PASSAGE (continued from First Passage, above)

Der Ordenstand brachte ihm den erhófften Frieden nicht, vielmehr steigerte sich bei ihm (note d) die Mönchstugend sélbstanklagender Démut in Verbín-dung mit der Wíllkürnatur des ockamistíschen Gottesbegriffs und mit der Augustínischen Prädestinatiónslehre zu Unruhe und Verzwéiflung ... Insbe-sóndere erschréckte ihn der Begríff der Geréchtigkeit Gottes, wie er in der dogmátischen ... Literatúr der Scholástik dem Begríff der Liebe ent-

gegengesetzt (note e), als strafende Tätigkeit Gottes erfasst ist, und
er fühlte nach den sakramentalen Absolutionen keine Änderung seines
sündhaften Zustands. Bei seinen Ordensbrüdern (note d) und Vorgesetzten
fand er wenig Verständnis. Doch tröstete ihn der Hinweis eines alten
Mönches auf das apostolische Bekenntnis: 'Ich glaube eine Vergebung der
Sünden': und von besonderem Wert war für ihn der Umgang mit Johann von
Staupitz, der als Ordensvikar auf ihn aufmerksam wurde und mit seiner
mystisch-evangelischen (note f) Frömmigkeit den fast schon 'Ersoffenen'
aus dem Wasser zog.

(Gustav Krüger, 'Reformation und Gegenreformation', in Handbuch der
Kirchengeschichte für Studierende. 3. Teil, 1909. Verlag von J.C.B.
Mohr (Paul Siebeck), Tübingen.)

Lesson XV

The concluding lessons of this course present longer extracts from German
theological works, but without special vocabulary lists. Readers should
consult the composite vocabulary at the end of the book. Grammatical notes
appear as before. The use of stress-marks is discontinued.

READING PASSAGE

Hesekiel versteht sich als ein Wächter (Hes. 33, 1-9; 3, 16b - 21). Es
ist seine Aufgabe, seine Landsleute zu warnen, wie ein Wächter die Bewohner
einer Stadt vor dem anrückenden Feind warnt. Wie der Wächter für das Leben
der Stadtbewohner verantwortlich ist, so trägt auch der Prophet eine ernste Verantwortung: er muss die warnende Botschaft Jahwes ungekürzt verkün-
digen. Seinen Hörern steht es frei, sie zu hören oder nicht zu hören
(note a). In dieser Anschauung ist bereits die Möglichkeit der Umkehr
mitgegeben (note b). Die näheren Voraussetzungen dafür (note c) werden
in der kleinen theologischen Abhandlung Kapitel 18 entfaltet. Es ist
nicht so, sagt Hesekiel, dass die Kinder für die Sünden der Väter zu leiden haben (note d); vielmehr steht die Möglichkeit der Umkehr jeder Gene-
ration offen. Jeder Mensch ist nur für sich selbst verantwortlich, ja
(note e), wenn er sich bekehrt, sind sogar seine früheren Sünden belanglos.
Ähnliche Gedanken sind auch von Jeremia geäussert worden, obwohl er den
neuen Grundsatz mit der Zeit des neuen Bundes verknüpft (Jer. 31, 29 f.).
Offenbar hat die Zeit Jeremias und Hesekiels das Individuum auf eine ganz
neue Weise entdeckt.

Die reinen Heilsweissagungen Hesekiels stammen vermutlich vorwiegend
aus der späteren Periode seines Wirkens, nach dem Fall Jerusalems. Wich-

tig ist, dass die Wiederaufrichtung Israels bei Hesekiel (note f) ganz
deutlich in die Kategorie des göttlichen Wunders hineingehört. In der
eindrucksvollen Vision von den toten Gebeinen sieht der Prophet, wie der
göttliche Geist in die Gebeine fährt und sie wider alle Erwartung lebendig
macht (Hes. 37, 1-14). So ist Israel zwar jetzt gestorben, kann aber
durch ein göttliches Wunder wieder aufgerichtet werden. (Eine Lehre von
der Auferstehung der Toten enthält dieser Abschnitt dagegen nicht)(note g).

In klaren Worten spricht Hesekiel seine Zukunftshoffnungen in Kapitel
36 aus. Die zerstreuten Kinder Israels werden aus allen Ländern heim-
kehren, das Land wird wieder bewohnt, die Städte werden befestigt und
die Äcker bestellt werden (note h), und Jahwe wird das Land mit Fruchtbarkeit segnen. Aber noch wichtiger ist dies: 'Ich werde euch mit
reinem Wasser besprengen, dass ihr rein werdet; von all eurer Unreinheit
und von all euren Götzen werde ich euch rein machen. Und ich werde euch
ein neues Herz geben und einen neuen Geist in euer Inneres legen; ich
werde das steinerne Herz aus eurem Leibe herausnehmen und euch ein
fleischernes Herz geben ... dass ihr in meinen Satzungen wandelt und
meine Gesetze treulich erfüllt ... und ihr werdet mein Volk sein, und
ich werde euer Gott sein' (36, 25 - 28).
Hier berührt sich Hesekiel an manchen Punkten mit Jeremia. Ein neuer
Gehorsam wird durch eine göttliche Neuschöpfung zustandegebracht. Die
Voraussetzung ist die Vergebung der Sünden (hier auf typisch priesterliche
Weise als rituelle Reinigung gedacht), und die Folge ist ein erneutes Bun-
desverhältnis, das hier wie bei Jeremia (note f) mit der alten Bundesformel
beschrieben wird. Bedeutsam ist bei Hesekiel aber, dass dies alles um
Jahwes heiligen Namens willen (note j) geschehen wird: 'Nicht um euretwillen (note k) handle ich (note l), Haus Israel, sondern für meinen heiligen Namen, den ihr entweiht habt unter den Völkern, zu denen (note m) ihr
gekommen seid. Ich werde meinen grossen Namen heiligen, der bei den Völkern entweiht ist ... und die Völker sollen erkennen, dass ich Jahwe bin,
wenn ich mich als heilig erweise vor ihren Augen' (36, 22f.).

Durch die Zerstörung Israels ist die Ehre Jahwes beeinträchtigt und
sein Name entweiht worden (note h). Jahwe muss für seine Ehre sorgen;
dadurch (note c) erweist er sich auch vor den Völkern als heilig, indem
sie erkennen müssen, dass er der mächtige Gott ist.

Als Führer des neuen Israels erscheint ein neuer David, der Fürst und
Hirte sein soll (34, 23f.; 37, 25ff.).

(Helmer Ringgren, _Israelitische Religion_. W. Kohlhammer Verlag, Stuttgart, 1963. S. 263-264.) (English edition: _Israelite Religion_. SPCK, 1966.)

GRAMMATICAL NOTES

a. Seinen Hörern steht es frei, sie zu hören oder nicht zu hören
  'His hearers are free to hear it or not to hear it'.

b. In dieser Anschauung ist bereits die Möglichkeit der Umkehr mitgegeben
  'In this view (of things) the possibility of conversion is already
  implicit'.

c. dafür, 'for it' (i.e. for conversion); dadurch, 'through this' (i.e.
  through Yahweh's being solicitous for His honour, sc. so restoring
  Israel to their land)

i. the following constructions are reminiscent of archaisms in English such as 'thereon', 'therewith', etc.:

damít 'with it', 'with them' (but not used in reference to <u>persons</u>)
dadúrch 'through it', 'through them' (but not used in reference to <u>persons</u>)
daráuf 'on it', 'on them' (but not used in reference to <u>persons</u>)
N.B. if the preposition begins with a vowel, -r- is inserted, e.g. darauf, darin, darunter

ii. If the meaning is, e.g., 'through <u>this/these</u>', the stress falls on da(<u>r</u>):

dádurch 'through this', through these'
dárauf 'on this', 'on these'.

<u>d</u>. ... die Kinder (<u>haben</u>) nicht ... <u>zu leiden</u> ('the children do not have to suffer ...')

This construction, precisely parallel to the English, should be noted. <u>Haben ... zu</u> is in most cases equivalent to, or slightly less strong than, <u>müssen</u>, and often emphasizes a <u>moral</u> obligation.

<u>e</u>. <u>ja</u>

In addition to its normal meaning of 'yes' <u>ja</u> has various other meanings and uses. In <u>spoken</u> German it is commonly found as a particle lending <u>emphasis</u> to a statement, e.g.:

Sagen Sie das <u>ja</u> nicht! 'Don't say that, whatever you do! (<u>ja</u> stressed)

Da <u>ist</u> er ja! 'Why, there he is!' (<u>ja</u> unstressed)

In <u>written</u> German, <u>stressed ja</u> frequently means 'indeed' (as in the relevant sentence from the text), while <u>unstressed ja</u> frequently means 'after all', i.e. it indicates something assumed to be obvious, e.g.:

Hesekiel konnte über den neuen Bund nicht so viel wissen wie wir, da Christus ja noch nicht gekommen war, 'Ezekiel could not know as much about the new covenant as we do, since <u>after all</u> Christ had not yet come.'

<u>f</u>. <u>bei Hesekiel</u>

For this use of <u>bei</u>, see Lesson XIV, note <u>d</u>.

<u>g</u>. <u>Eine Lehre ... enthält dieser Abschnitt dagegen nicht</u> ('this passage does not, on the other hand, contain any doctrine ...')

Note the effect produced by inverting word order: by placing the direct object <u>first</u> in the sentence, the writer gives it great prominence, as if anticipating the possible question: 'Does not this passage contain the doctrine of the resurrection of the dead?'

<u>h</u>. <u>das Land wird wieder bewohnt, die Städte werden befestigt und die Äcker bestellt werden</u>

All these three clauses are in the future passive, i.e. the final <u>werden</u> covers them all. A similar construction occurs towards the end of this passage, where, in the <u>perfect</u> passive, <u>worden</u> covers two clauses. Cf. Lesson XIV, note <u>e</u>.

<u>j</u>. <u>um Jahwes heiligen Namens willen</u>

Where an adjective occurs before a noun but without any preceding arti-

cle, etc., the adjective normally takes the ending that would have been
on the definite article, had one been present (Lesson VIII, note c).
This does not apply, however, in the masc. and neut. gen., where the
adjective takes not -es but -en. Further e.g.: ein Glas kalten
Wassers, 'a glass of cold water'.

k. um euretwillen ('for your sakes')

cf. the similar formations:
      um meinetwillen 'for my sake'
      um deinetwillen 'for thy sake'
      um seinetwillen 'for his sake', etc.

l. handle ich

This is the 1st person singular of handeln, 'to act'. If the stem of a
verb ends in -el, the e of this syllable usually drops out in the first
person singular, cf. wandeln: ich wandle. But it reappears thereafter:
du wandelst, er wandelt, etc.

m. zu denen ihr gekommen seid ('to whom ye have come')

i. The following is a complete table of the relative pronoun. (Note
its similarity to the definite article, apart from the dat. plural
and the whole of the gen.):

	M.	F.	N.	PL.
Nom.	der	die	das	die
Acc.	den	die	das	die
Gen.	DESSEN	DEREN	DESSEN	DEREN
Dat.	dem	der	dem	DENEN

ii. The above forms are also used as emphatic or demonstrative pronouns, e.g. Wer an mich glaubt, der hat das ewige Leben.

iii. In certain circumstances, derer is found instead of deren, e.g.
Lesson X, note l.

Lesson XVI

READING PASSAGE

Die jüdische Diaspora in Ägypten übernahm bald hellenistische Kultur und
griechische Sprache. So wurde eine Übersetzung der Heiligen Schriften ins
Griechische erforderlich. Etwa um die Mitte des 3. Jahrhunderts wurde
damit begonnen. Die Legende erzählt, sie sei von 72 Männern in 72 Wochen

geschaffen worden; deshalb wurde sie gewöhnlich als Septuaginta ('siebzig') bezeichnet.

Die Septuaginta ist eine äusserst interessante religionsgeschichtliche Quelle, da sie 'wie jede nicht eigentlich gelehrte Übersetzung eine Umsetzung in eine neue geistige Welt ist' und in zahlreichen Fällen eine gewisse Angleichung und Anpassung an das griechische Denken erkennen lässt (note a). Man hat sogar von einer besonderen 'Septuaginta-Frömmigkeit' gesprochen. So ist z.B. (zum Beispiel) eine Tendenz zur Milderung der Anthropomorphismen und des Irrationalen im Gottesbild zu beobachten (note a). Der Gottesname Jahwe wird zu (note b) Kurios, 'der Herr', oder, wie Ex. 3, 14 'der Seiende' (note c); die Epitheta Schaddai und Zebaoth werden durch Pantokrator, 'Allherrscher', versetzt. Menschliche Reaktionen wie Zorn und Reue erscheinen Gott unangemessen (note d). So wird der Gottesbegriff der Vernunft einsichtig (note d) gemacht und die Unveränderlichkeit und Transzendenz Gottes werden hervorgehoben. Die Sünde wird gern als frevelhafter Übermut oder Hybris charakterisiert. Die Ethik der Sprüche wird mittels kleiner Änderungen der griechischen Gedankenwelt annehmbar gemacht. Der Auferstehungsglaube wird manchen Textstellen untergelegt. Noch viele andere Beispiele für diese Tendenz könnten beigebracht werden, aber die genannten dürften (note e) die allgemeine Art der Anpassung genügend deutlich machen. In Einzelheiten bleibt auf diesem Felde noch vieles zu erforschen.

Auch die griechische Philosophie hat das ägyptische Judentum beeinflusst. Eine hervorragende Gestalt jüdischen Denkens (note f) auf ägyptischem Boden ist Philo von Alexandrien (etwa 20 v. Chr. bis 45 n. Chr. (zwanzig vor Christo bis fünfundvierzig nach Christo)). Bei ihm hat sich griechisches, besonders stoisches und platonisches Denken mit dem Glauben des Judentums zu einer Einheit vermählt (note b). Die Gedanken der Philosophie werden mittels allegorischer Exegese in den Pentateuch hineingelesen.

Dass Gott der Schöpfer der Welt ist, steht für Philo fest (note g). Aber er verknüpft diesen Gedanken mit der platonischen Ideenlehre und mit der stoischen Lehre von der Weltvernunft oder dem Logos. Am ersten Schöpfungstag konzipierte Gott demgemäss in seinen Gedanken oder in seiner Vernunft (Logos) die Ideenwelt, d.h. (das heisst) die gedachte Welt, das Vorbild der sinnlich wahrnehmbaren Welt. Letzten Endes (note f) ist der Logos aber auch mit der Weisheit und mit dem offenbarten Gesetz identisch. Gott wirkt in der Welt durch Kräfte (dynameis), die am Logos Anteil haben. Gelegentlich setzt Philo sie mit den Engeln gleich.

Der Mensch ist ein Abbild eines himmlischen Menschen oder des Logos. Er besitzt einen sterblichen Körper und eine unsterbliche Seele. Auf diese Weise nimmt er eine Mittelstellung zwischen dem Göttlichen und der materiellen Welt ein. In der Welt lebt er in Unwissenheit und Ungehorsam; aber er kann durch Vermittlung des Logos Anteil an Gott gewinnen. Die biblische Offenbarung, das Gesetz, das im Grunde mit der Weltordnung identisch ist, führt den Menschen auf den Weg zur Vollkommenheit. Durch Übung und Wissen kann er sich Gott nähern; wirkliche Gemeinschaft mit ihm erlangt er jedoch nur durch den Glauben (pistis), d.h. durch das Überzeugtsein (note h) von Gottes Existenz und das Vertrauen auf seine Vorsehung.
So vertritt also Philo eine Synthese von Offenbarungsreligion und Philosophie, die, obwohl ihre Form hellenistisch anmutet, im Grunde genommen doch als jüdisch anzusprechen ist. Auf die Dauer hat sich allerdings die aus den Lehren der Pharisäer hervorgegangene Theologie als lebenskräftiger als das spekulative System Philos erwiesen (note j).

(Helmer Ringgren, op. cit., S. 316-318.)

GRAMMATICAL NOTES

<u>a</u>. i. läßt ... erkennen, 'allows ... <u>to be recognized</u>'

   ii. eine Tendenz ... (ist) zu beóbachten, 'a tendency ... <u>is to be</u>
       <u>observed</u>'
       Note that in both cases an <u>active</u> infinitive in German requires
       to be translated by a <u>passive</u> infinitive in English. Cf. Lesson
       XI, note <u>e</u>.

<u>b</u>. wird <u>zu</u>. Cf. Lesson XII, note <u>f</u>. ii.

   hat sich ... <u>zu</u> einer Einheit vermählt, 'has become wedded ... to form
   a unity'.

<u>c</u>. <u>der Seiende</u>, lit. 'the Being One'
   <u>seiend</u> is the (very rare) present participle of <u>sein</u>, 'to be'.

<u>d</u>. i. <u>Gott unangemessen</u>, 'inappropriate for God'
       (<u>Gott</u> is dative; cf. Lesson XIII, note <u>b</u>). <u>Unangemessen</u> follows
       <u>Gott</u> because it is strictly a past participle (from <u>an/messen</u>,
       to adapt, suit)

   ii. <u>der Vernunft einsichtig</u>, 'intelligible to reason'
       <u>einsichtig</u> is one of a large number of adjectives which follow a
       qualifying phrase. In general these adjectives are such as derive
       from <u>verbs</u>, thus: einsichtig derives from Einsicht (insight), which
       is connected with ein/sehen, 'to understand', 'perceive'. Cf. <u>ver-</u>
       <u>antwortlich</u> in Lesson XV: Jeder Mensch ist nur für sich selbst
       <u>verantwortlich</u>, 'Each person is responsible only for himself.'
       The basic verb here is <u>verantworten</u>, 'to answer for'.

<u>e</u>. ... <u>Beispiele</u> ... <u>könnten</u> beigebracht werden, aber die genannten
   <u>dürften</u> ..., ' ... examples <u>could(might)</u> be adduced, but those named
   <u>should(ought to)</u> ...'

   Here is an example of the 'tentative' use of the imperfect subjunctive, and also of the wide range of meanings of the auxiliary verbs
   <u>können</u>, <u>dürfen</u>. For accurate understanding, particularly of the
   subjunctive forms of these verbs, frequent reference to a good
   dictionary is essential at first.

<u>f</u>. <u>jüdischen Denkens</u>, 'of Jewish thought'; <u>letzten Endes</u>, 'in the final
   analysis'
   For this adjective ending, see Lesson XV, note <u>j</u>.

<u>g</u>. .... steht für Philo <u>fest</u>, 'Philo is utterly convinced'.

<u>h</u>. <u>das Überzeugtsein</u>, 'being convinced'. Cf. Lesson XI, note <u>h</u>.

<u>j</u>. die ... Theologie ... hat sich <u>als</u> lebenskräftiger <u>als</u> das System ...
   <u>erwiesen</u>, (lit.) 'showed itself <u>as</u> more vigorous <u>than</u> ...'

I

   Die Bergpredigt ist also nicht, das ist unser bisheriges Ergebnis, die
Wiedergabe einer zusammenhängenden Predigt Jesu, so wenig wie die Gleich-
nisrede Mt. (Matthäus) 13, sondern ist eine Sammlung von Jesusworten. Zu
welchem Zweck wurde diese Sammlung veranstaltet? Wie kam man darauf?
(note a) Hier ist es hilfreich, wenn wir uns an ein Resultat der Arbeiten
des bekannten englischen Neutestamentlers C.H. Dodd erinnern, der die
grundliegende Beobachtung gemacht hat, dass es in der ältesten Zeit überall in der Christenheit eine zweifache Form der Predigt gegeben hat
(note b), nämlich Verkündigung und Lehre, Kerygma und Didache. Diese
beiden Begriffe werden unglücklicherweise ständig durcheinandergeworfen,
obwohl jeder von ihnen, jedenfalls nach paulinischem Sprachgebrauch, etwas
ganz Verschiedenes (note c) bezeichnet. Verkündigung, Kerygma, ist die
missionarische Predigt an Juden und Heiden. Inhalt der missionarischen
Predigt war die Botschaft vom gekreuzigten und auferstandenen Herrn und
von seiner Wiederkunft. Die älteste Zusammenfassung des Kerygmas steht 1.
Kor. 15, 3-5: 'Jesus ist gestorben für unsere Sünden nach der Schrift und
begraben worden. Aber Gott hat ihn auferweckt am dritten Tage nach der
Schrift, und er ist Kephas erschienen, danach den Zwölfen' (notes a, d).
Also die Verkündigung von Christus, die Botschaft, dass er uns versöhnt
hat und unser Friede ist, das ist das Kerygma. Vom Kerygma zu unterscheiden ist die Didache, die Lehre, die Predigt an die Gemeinde. Wendet
sich das Kerygma nach aussen, so die Didache nach innen. Jeder Gottes-
dienst begann mit der Didache. Apg. (Apostelgeschichte) 2, 42 haben wir,
würde ich meinen (note e), die Schilderung des Ablaufs eines urchristlichen Gottesdienstes (note f) vor uns. Er bestand aus vier Teilen.
Den Anfang bildete (note g) 1) die Lehre (Didache) der Apostel, dann
folgte 2) die Koinonia (worunter wahrscheinlich die Tischgemeinschaft
zu verstehen ist)(note h); hieran schloss sich 3) das Brotbrechen, die
Eucharistie an, und den Abschluss bildete 4) die Gebete. Die Lehre, die
Unterweisung steht also am Anfang des Gottesdienstes, und dafür (note a)
haben wir auch sonst zahlreiche Belege.

(Joachim Jeremias, Abba. Studien zur neutestamentlichen Theologie und
Zeitgeschichte. Vandenhoeck und Ruprecht, Göttingen, 1966. S. 180-181.)

II

   Die Frage, ob die Überlieferung der Worte Jesu oder die der Geschichten von ihm früher zu festen Formen gelangt ist, scheint mir kein debat-
tierbares wissenschaftliches Problem zu sein. Die Bedürfnisse der
Gemeinde, die zu beiden Überlieferungen Anlass gegeben haben, werden
sich gleichzeitig geltend gemacht haben, und die Erkenntnis dieser
Bedürfnisse ist jedenfalls das fassbare und wesentliche Problem. Nur
darf man m.E. (meines Erachtens) nicht einseitig konstruktiv verfahren
und aus dem - wenn auch vielleicht mit Recht - vorausgesetzten Gemeinde-
bedürfnissen die Formen der Überlieferung einfach ableiten. Sondern

Konstruktion und Analyse müssen in Wechselbeziehung stehen ... Und was
den Ausgangspunkt betrifft, so ziehe ich jetzt vor, analytisch vorzugehen
und aus dem Charakter der Überlieferungsstücke auf ihren 'Sitz im Leben',
ihren Entstehungs- und Pflegeort (note j) in der Gemeinde zu schliessen,
wodurch (note h) freilich das Verständnis ihrer Form vervollständigt wird.

Ob man mit den Worten oder Geschichten beginnt, scheint mir also eine
sekundäre Frage zu sein; ich beginne mit den Worten. Ich rechne aber unter
die Wortüberlieferung eine Gattung von Traditionsstücken, die man versucht
sein könnte, zu den Geschichten zu zählen, nämlich solche Stücke, deren
Pointe ein in einen kurzen Rahmen gefasstes Jesuswort bildet (note k). Ich
nenne sie mit einem in der griechischen Literaturgeschichte gebräuchlichen
und möglichst neutralen Terminus 'Apophthegmata'. Dass ich die Apophthegmata vor den rahmenlosen Jesusworten behandle (note l), wird der Verlauf
der Untersuchung rechtfertigen. Der Hauptgrund (note m) ist aber, dass
manche Apophthegmata durch die Erkenntnis vom sekundären Charakter ihres
Rahmens auf Herrenworte reduziert werden, die dann im folgenden Teil mit den
anderen Herrenworten zusammen betrachtet werden müssen.

(Rudolf Bultmann, Die Geschichte der synoptischen Tradition. 2. Auflage.
Vandenhoeck und Ruprecht, Göttingen, 1931. S. 8.)

GRAMMATICAL NOTES

a. Wie kam man daráuf? ('How was it arrived at?'); dánach ('after this');
dáfür ('for this')

For these forms cf. Lesson XV, note c.

b. es hat gegeben ('there has been', 'there was')

Note this very important phrase. It is always 3rd person singular, and
takes the acc. case. Its tenses are those of the strong verb geben,
'to give'; i.e.

Pres.	es gibt	'there is/are'
Imp.	es gab	'there was/were'
Perf.	es hat gegeben	'there has/have been'
Pluperf.	es hatte gegeben	'there had been'
Fut.	es wird geben	'there will be'

c. etwas Verschiedenes ('something different')

For this construction, cf. Lesson XI, note f.

d. den Zwölfen ('to the twelve')

In older German, numbers were normally declined. Today, however, only
the number 'one' declines - like the indefinite article (see Lesson IX,
note c).

e. ich würde meinen ('I would think')

Care is needed in translating meinen; see Lesson XIII, Vocabulary II.

f. eines urchristlichen Gottesdienstes ('of an early Christian service')

The use of the prefix ur- should be noted. It is found both on adjec-

tives and on nouns, and usually denotes primitiveness, origin or
extreme antiquity, e.g.:

urchristlich	early Christian	der Urtext	original text
das Urchristentum	primitive Christianity	die Urform	original form
der Ursprung	origin	uralt	ancient
ursprünglich	original	der Urmensch	primitive man
die Urgeschichte	primeval history	der Urgrossvater	great-grand-father
der Urwald	primeval forest		
		die Ursache	cause

g. <u>Den Anfang bildete</u>

For this inverted construction, see Lesson XV, note <u>g</u>.

h. <u>worunter</u> wahrscheinlich die Tischgemeinschaft <u>zu verstehen ist</u> ('by
which, probably, table fellowship is to be understood')

  i. <u>verstehen unter</u> ... = 'to understand <u>by</u> ....

  ii. <u>worunter</u> is the 'relative' equivalent of <u>darunter</u> (cf. note <u>a</u>),
i.e. it corresponds to English 'where-'; e.g.:

      womit   'wherewith', i.e. 'with which'
      wodurch   'by means of which'
      worauf   'whereon', i.e. 'on which', etc.

  iii. <u>ist zu verstehen</u>, see Lesson XVI, note <u>a</u>. ii

j. <u>ihren Entstehungs- und Pflegeort</u> ('their place of origin and the place
where they were fostered')

The hyphen indicates that -<u>ort</u> (der Ort, 'place') belongs to the end of
this word too.

k. <u>deren Pointe</u> ('whose point') <u>ein in einen kurzen Rahmen gefasstes Jesuswort bildet</u>
'the whole point of which is (formed by) a saying of Jesus enclosed in a
brief framework')

  i. For the relative pronoun <u>deren</u>, see Lesson XV, note <u>m</u>.

  ii. There are occasions when the English passive is the best way to
translate a German active construction.

l. <u>ich ... behandle</u>

1st person singular of <u>behandeln</u>. See Lesson XV, note <u>l</u>.

m. <u>der Hauptgrund</u> ('the main reason')

Note this use of <u>Haupt-</u> in the sense of 'main', 'chief'. Further
examples:

      die Hauptquelle   'main source', 'fountain-head'
      die Hauptstadt   'capital city'
      der Hauptmann   'captain'

Lesson XVIII

Lesson XVIII

READING PASSAGES

<u>I</u>

(In the early years of this century two Armenian scholars, Dr Karapet Ter-Mekerttschian and Dr Erwand Ter-Minassiantz, discovered and translated into German Irenaeus' tract <u>Epideixis</u>. The following passage is from Adolf Harnack's epilogue (Nachwort) to the translation's 2nd edition, published in 1908 by J.C. Hinrichs'sche Buchhandlung, Leipzig, under the title: <u>Des heiligen Irenäus Schrift zum Erweise der apostolischen Verkündigung</u>)

Wir erfahren, wie bemerkt, aus der Schrift (note <u>a</u>) kaum etwas, was wir nicht schon wüssten (note <u>b</u>), und doch ist ihre Entdeckung von hoher Wichtigkeit (note <u>c</u>). Wir lernen aus ihr, wie fest und lebendig dem Irenäus die Gedanken waren, die er in 'Adversus haereses' entwickelt hat. 'Adv. haer.' ist eine polemisch-dogmatisch-wissenschaftliche Schrift, auch an einen Freund gerichtet, aber diesem Freund wird ein weitschichtiger, komplizierter Stoff und ein nicht geringes Mass von Denkarbeit zugemutet (note <u>d</u>); unser Traktat ist katechetisch erbaulich und stellt viel geringere Anforderungen an den Leser. Aber alle Hauptpunkte der Religionslehre in 'Adv. haer.' finden sich auch hier: sie waren dem Irenäus nicht Theologie, sondern die Religion selbst, und dies von seinem Standpunkt aus mit Recht. Ein jedes Gemeindemitglied sollte sie kennen (note <u>e</u>) und auch der Häresie gegenüber (note <u>f</u>) seinen Glauben zu verteidigen vermögen. Irenäus lebt wirklich mit ganzem Gemüt, mit dem Kopf und mit dem Herzen (note <u>g</u>), in dem Glauben der Kirche, wie er ihn sich zentralisiert und verständlich gemacht hat (note <u>h</u>), und er weiss diesem Glauben (trotz dem ungeheuren Apparat)(note <u>j</u>) seine Einfachheit und Kraft, seine praktische Abzweckung und Wärme zu erhalten. Es ist doch ein grosser Eindruck, den man empfängt: so ist in Lyon am Ende des 2. (zweiten) Jahrhunderts die Christenheit unterwiesen und geleitet worden! Hierarchisches und Zeremonielles (note <u>k</u>) fehlt ganz, ja letzteres wird aufs entschiedenste abgelehnt. Alles liegt in der Sphäre des Geistes, der Wahrheit, der Gesinnung, der sittlichen Tat; die Kirchenautorität und Tradition wird gar nicht in Szene gesetzt; der biblische Beweis genügt. Auch das Sakramentale, welches nicht fehlt, tritt doch zurück. Die 'Heilstatsachen' zersplittern und belasten die Einheit und Freiheit noch nicht; sie sind alle in Eins zusammengeschlossen. In dieser Hinsicht vermag Irenäus wohl mit Clemens Alexandrinus und Origenes zu rivalisieren, wenn er auch (note <u>l</u>) die wissenschaftliche Methode nicht besass, um seiner Religion und Dogmatik die Freiheit zu erhalten. Aber die Leser empfingen in dem Büchlein einen Schatz und zugleich ein Manuale biblicum, eine Sammlung zweckmässig ausgewählter Stellen aus dem Alten Testament, die ihnen die Lektüre des weitschichtigen Buches ('Adv. haer.') etwas ersetzen konnte. Auch wir lesen heute das ganze Büchlein mit Respekt und einzelne Abschnitte mit Bewunderung und innerer Bewegung.

II

Eben in seiner O f f e n b a r u n g, eben in J e s u s C h r i s t u s,
hat sich ja der verborgene Gott fassbar gemacht. Nicht direkt, sondern
indirekt. Nicht für das Schauen, sondern für den Glauben. Nicht in seinem
Wesen, aber im Zeichen. Nicht unter **Aufhebung seiner Verborgenheit** also -
aber fassbar! Das ist ja Gottes Offenbarung: dass Gott der von ihm er-
wählten und dazu bestimmten Kreatur den Auftrag und die Macht gegeben hat,
ihn zu vertreten und darzustellen, von ihm Zeugnis abzulegen. Das Wort
ward Fleisch (note m): das ist das erste, ursprüngliche und regierende
Zeichen aller Zeichen. Auf dieses Zeichen hin, als Zeichen dieses Zeichen,
gibt es eine kreatürliche Bezeugung seines ewigen Wortes auch sonst, nicht
überall, aber da, wo dieses sein ewiges Wort sich selbst seine Zeugen er-
wählt, berufen und geschaffen hat: ein Bezeugen durch das Wort der Propheten und Apostel dieses Wortes, durch die sichtbare Existenz seines
Volkes, seiner Kirche, durch die Botschaft, die da ausgerichtet wird und
zu vernehmen ist, durch die Sakramente, in denen diese Botschaft ihre auch
physisch sichtbare und greifbare Gestalt hat, durch unsere, der an diese
Zeugnisse Glaubenden, Existenz endlich (note n).

Jesus Christus und sein sichtbares Reich auf Erden: das ist die grosse,
von Gott selbst geschaffene Möglichkeit, ihn anzusehen und zu begreifen
und also auch von ihm zu reden - so, wie wir Menschen ihn anschauen und
begreifen, so, wie wir von ihm reden können, nicht ohne die Hülle, nicht
ohne den Vorbehalt seiner Verborgenheit also, nicht ausserhalb des Wunders
seiner Gnade.

Es ist nicht so, dass die Gnade seiner Offenbarung je und in irgend
einer Beziehung aufhörte (note b), Gnade und Wunder zu sein, nicht so,
dass Gott selbst und sein freies Handeln je überflüssig würde (note b),
weil wir an seiner Stelle die von ihm erwählte und bestimmte Kreatur
hätten (note b). Es ist aber auch nicht so, dass wir Menschen nun
doch uns selbst überlassen wären (note b): der Unwissenheit oder unseres
eigenen Herzens Erfindung (note g). Es ist vielmehr so, dass wir als
Menschen und im Raume unserer menschlichen Anschauungen und Begriffe
eine von Gott selbst ausgehende, seinem Willen entsprechende und mit
seiner Verheissung versehene Weisung haben, auf Grund und nach Anwei-
sung derer (note o) wir ihn anschauen und begreifen dürfen und sollen,
auf Grund und nach Anleitung derer nun auch in menschlichen Worten von
dem verborgenen Gott geredet werden darf und soll (note p).

(Karl Barth, Die Kirchliche Dogmatik, 2. Band. 2. Auflage. Evange-
lischer Verlag A.G. Zollikon-Zürich, 1946. S. 223-224.)

GRAMMATICAL NOTES

a. aus der Schrift ('from this work', sc. of Irenaeus)

> For the wide range of meanings covered by Schrift, see Vocabulary
> of Lesson IV.

b. kaum etwas, was wir nicht schon wüssten ('hardly anything which we
did not know already');
nicht so, dass Gott ... überflüssig würde ('not that God becomes
superfluous')

> An imperfect or pluperfect subjunctive is sometimes found associated
> with a negative statement. It expresses a nuance of meaning which can

hardly be reproduced in English, and it should therefore be translated by an indicative, in whatever tense is appropriate. Notice, in
the Karl Barth passage, how all the imperfect subjunctives after the
negative (es ist) nicht so ..., give way to indicatives after the tone
changes to the positive es ist vielmehr so ....

c. von hoher Wichtigkeit ('of great (lit. high) importance')

The adjective hoch loses its c in declension, and also in its comparative: höher.

d. diesem Freund wird ein weitschichtiger, komplizierter Stoff und ein
nicht geringes Mass von Denkarbeit zugemutet: 'this friend is expected
(to cope with) a vast (quantity of) complicated material and (to be
capable of) no meagre amount of brainwork'

e. Ein jedes Gemeindemitglied sollte sie kennen ('every single church member ought to know them')

  i. ein jedes is much more emphatic than jedes.
  ii. Mitglied ('member') is neuter, even when referring to a person.
  It is formed from das Glied(er), 'limb'.
  iii. sollte is imperf. subj. of sollen (cf. Lessons VII. 2; XX. f.).

f. der Häresie gegenüber ('in face of heresy')
gegenüber normally means 'opposite'; always takes dat.; and usually
follows its noun.

g. dem Herzen; unseres ... Herzens

das Herz declines in the following irregular manner:

	singular	plural
Nom.	das Herz	die Herzen
Acc.	das Herz	die Herzen
Gen.	des Herzens	der Herzen
Dat.	dem Herzen	den Herzen

h. wie er ihn sich zentralisiert und verständlich gemacht hat, 'as he has
concentrated it and made it intelligible to his own mind'.

i. trotz dem ungeheuren Apparat ('in spite of the enormous amount of
material')

  i. trotz is found with both gen. and dat. Nowadays gen. is commoner,
  though in the adverb trotzdem, 'nevertheless', the dat. (dem) still
  persists.
  ii. ungeheuer (and other adjectives in -auer, -euer) tend to lose the
  final e of their stem in declension, e.g.:

    sauer, 'sour': saure Milch, 'sour milk'
    teuer, 'dear', 'expensive': ein teurer Freund, 'a dear friend'
  The same is true of adjectives in -el, e.g.:
    edel, 'noble': ein edler Mensch, 'a noble person'
    dunkel, 'dark': eine dunkle Nacht, 'a dark night'
  This principle holds also in the comparative, e.g.:
    ein edlerer Mensch, 'a nobler person'

<u>k</u>. <u>Hierarchisches und Zeremonielles</u> ('hierarchical and ceremonial matters')

The final -<u>es</u> on the adjectives indicates the neuter singular, i.e.
'(that which is) hierarchical'.

<u>l</u>. wenn ... <u>auch</u> ('<u>even</u> if ...')

Note this important second meaning of <u>auch</u>, 'even'. Further e.g.:
<u>Auch</u> im Alten Testament findet man die Lehre von der Auferstehung der
Toten.

<u>m</u>. Das Wort <u>ward</u> Fleisch ('the Word became flesh')

Luther's version of Jn. 1:14 has an abiding place in modern German,
despite the now archaic imperfect of <u>werden</u>. Normally, modern German
would require <u>wurde</u>.

<u>n</u>. durch unsere, der an diese Zeugnisse Glaubenden, Existenz endlich
'Finally through our existence, (the existence, that is) of those who
believe in these testimonies'

<u>o</u>. <u>auf Grund und nach Anweisung derer</u> ... ('on the basis, and according to
the directions, of which ...') Cf. Lesson XV, note <u>m</u>. iii.

<u>p</u>. <u>auch in menschlichen Worten von dem verborgenen Gott geredet werden
darf und soll</u>
'the hidden God (not only) may (but) should be talked about, even in
human words'.

Lesson XIX

READING PASSAGES

<u>I</u>

Der Pietismus wollte ... das kirchliche Bekenntnis (obschon er seine
abweichende Lehreigentümlichkeit hatte), in seiner vollen Geltung lassen;
allein er hob hervor, dass zum grossen Schaden des kirchlichen Lebens
der Rechtgläubigkeit diejenige Bedeutung beigelegt werde, die doch nur
dem innerlichen, den Menschen wirklich erneuenden Glauben zukommen könnte (note <u>a</u>), dass Rechtgläubigkeit und Frömmigkeit zwei ganz verschie-
dene Dinge wären, dass aber Frömmigkeit den Menschen vor allem Not tue,
indem die R e l i g i o n wesentlich S a c h e d e s H e r z e n s sei.

Der Pietismus fasste also die Religion nicht als Zustimmung zur Lehre
der Kirche und als Wandel in den Ordnungen der Kirche, sondern als ein
wesentlich innerliches Leben, als Herzensleben auf.

Dasselbe (note a) wird nach der übereinstimmenden Lehre aller Pietisten durch die Vereinigung des Menschen mit Christus begründet. Die reformierte Lehre von der 'insitio' des Menschen in Christum wird daher auch von Spener vertreten: 'Nicht nur Christi Kraft und Geist, sondern Christus selbst vereinigt sich wahrhaftig mit den Gläubigen, dass sie seine Glieder so wahrhaftig sind, als er ihr Haupt ist' (note b).

Hierdurch wird der spezifische Unterschied des bekehrten von dem unbekehrten, des wiedergeborenen von dem natürlichen Menschen begründet. Der Wiedergeborene allein wandelt im Lichte Gottes, indem der Geist ihn innerlich im Herzen einleuchtet, so dass er die Geheimnisse der Offenbarung wirklich erfahren, wirklich verstehen kann, während der natürliche Mensch nur die Worte der Offenbarung, nicht aber deren Sinn versteht (note c). Daher kann nur ein wiedergeborener Christ wirklich Theologe und Lehrer des Evangeliums sein. Ein Theologe, der nicht wiedergeboren ist, ist nur ein Kenner des Buchstabens (note d), nicht aber des Geistes.

Mit begeisterter Rede wird von allen Pietisten die Herrlichkeit des Christenlebens, der Friede und die Freude, mit der es erfüllt (note e), die Geisteskraft, mit der es gesalbt ist, verkündet.

Da der Glaube im Sinne des Pietismus wesentlich t ä t i g e r G l a u b e ist, so fassen die Pietisten die Rechtfertigung so auf (note f), dass sie, als Vereinigung des Menschen mit Christus, der wesentliche Anfang der Heiligung ist. Daher ist der Glaube durch sich selbst (note g) fruchtbar in guten Werken. Indem daher der Fleiss in der Heiligung ein wesentliches Kennzeichen der Rechtfertigung ist, so kann das Leben des Gerechtfertigten, nur als ein im Glauben und in der Heiligung w a c h s e n d e s Leben gedacht werden.

Gern wird das Leben des Christen von den Pietisten unter dem Gesichtspunkte der Nachfolge Jesu betrachtet. Der Christ soll Christo im Leben und im Leiden immer ähnlicher zu werden suchen. Daher hat der Christ alles Kreuz der Lebens (Anfechtung, Heimsuchen, Verfolgung, Krankheit, Armut, u.s.w.)(und so weiter) nicht bloss als Strafe, sondern auch zur Übung (note h) seines Gehorsams gegen Gott nach dem Vorbilde Jesu in rechter Gottergebenheit zu tragen (note j).

(H. Heppe, 'Das Wesen und der Unterschied von Mystik und Pietismus', the introduction (Einleitung) to his Geschichte des Pietismus und der Mystik in der Reformierten Kirche namentlich der Niederlande. E.J. Brill, Leiden, 1879.)

II

Die Bekehrung bedeutet das durch Gottes Wort in Gesetz und Evangelium gewirkte völlige Nein zu meinem sündhaften Sein und das völlige Ja zu Gottes gnädigem Annehmen meiner selbst (note k), des Sünders; Preisgabe an Gottes Gericht, Preisgabe an seine vergebende Gnade, totale Absage und totale Hingabe. Sie ist demnach Bekehrung zum Glauben im Sinne der fides specialis oder salvifica, der bedingungslosen Gründung des Lebens auf Gottes wunderbare Zusage seiner Barmherzigkeit allein. Die Bekehrung ist also viel mehr als eine ethische Wandlung oder Umkehr, etwa die Wendung aus ethischer Laxheit oder Verwahrlosung zum sittlichen Ernste, von der Verachtung der Gebote Gottes zum Gehorsam gegen sie. Eine solche ethische Bekehrung ist auch ohne Christus und das Evangelium möglich und nicht selten geschehen - zu ihr braucht man Jesus Christus nicht. Die Bekehrung im christlichen Sinne wird im konkreten Falle auch

ethische Bekehrung einschliessen, aber durchaus nicht in jedem Falle, wie
das Beispiel des Apostels Paulus zeigt: sie kann auch Bekehrung eines
'guten Menschen', eines Pharisäers, also eines ethisch Hochstehenden sein.
Auch dann ist sie die Bekehrung eines Sünders. Aber die Sünde ist dann nicht
der Mangel an Ethos, sondern der falsche Ton des Ethos, gerade auf seiner
Höhe, das 'Aufrichten der eigenen Gerechtigkeit' (Röm. 10,3), also die
Sünde wider das erste Gebot. Die Bekehrung in diesem Sinne hat metaethi-
schen Charakter, und eben damit ist sie ein völliges Neuwerden des Menschen,
neue Geburt. Der Mensch ist nun aus dem Unglauben in den Glauben gekommen,
aus der unethischen oder ethischen Selbstherrlichkeit und Sicherheit in
das demütige Sichgründen (note l) auf die Gnade allein; aus dem Vertrauen
auf das eigene Ethos in das Lebenwollen (note l) allein von Gottes Huld
in Christus. Das bedeutet eine Wandlung des Lebens in seiner Tiefe. Es
ist nicht zu verstehen als eine Stufe des Wachstums oder der Entwicklung,
nicht als ein blosser Durchbruch in grössere Tiefe, stärkerem Ernst; es
lässt sich nur bezeichnen (note m) als Bruch, als totale Wendung, aus dem
geistlichen Tode in das Leben.

(Paul Althaus, 'Die Bekehrung in reformatorischer und pietetischer Sicht',
in Neue Zeitschrift für systematische Theologie, 1. Band, 1959, Heft 1.
S. 5,6. Verlag Alfred Töpelmann, Berlin W.35.)

GRAMMATICAL NOTES

a. der Rechtgläubigkeit (werde) diejenige Bedeutung beigelegt, die doch
nur dem innerlichen, den Menschen wirklich erneuenden Glauben zukommen
könnte ('to orthodoxy (was) attributed that significance which, after
all, could belong only to inward faith, (the faith) which really
renews man')

   i. diejenige Bedeutung, die ..., 'that significance which ...'
     dasselbe 'the same' (neuter because referring to (das) Herzens-
     leben)
     While written as one word, these combinations decline as two words,
     i.e. definite article and adjective. Another such combination,
     dergleiche, 'the same', was given in Lesson XII, Vocabulary II.
     Derjenige, etc. is used for great emphasis, and is almost always
     followed, as here, by a relative clause.
   ii. werde; könnte
     These verbs are subjunctive because they form part of reported
     speech (see Lesson X), dependent on er hob hervor, 'it emphasized
     ...'. (For er in the sense of 'it', see Lesson VII, note f.)

b. dass sie seine Glieder so wahrhaftig sind, als er ihr Haupt ist
('that they are His members as truly as He is their head')

   i. so ... als
     Modern German would have so ... wie.
   ii. Haupt
     In Spener's day (1635-1705) this word was regularly used for 'head'
     in almost all its senses. It is still used in elevated style (e.g.
     gekrönte Häupter, 'crowned heads'; das Haupt der Gemeinde, 'the
     Head of the Church'), and its use in compounds (='main', 'chief')
     was described in Lesson XVII, note m. In its normal, literal
     sense it has now been replaced by der Kopf.

c. der natürliche Mensch (versteht) nur die Worte der Offenbarung, nicht aber deren Sinn (i.e. the meaning of the revelation)

This use of the gen. of the demonstrative pronoun, to restrict the reference to the last-named noun, was dealt with in Lesson XIV, note c.

d. des Buchstabens

Der Buchstabe, like der Friede, der Glaube, and der Name (see Lesson VII, note b. i), adds -ns in gen. singular, and -n in all other cases, singular and plural.

e. die Freude, mit der es erfüllt (ist)

The ist of the following clause is made to do duty for both clauses (cf. Lesson XIV, note e).

f. so fassen die Pietisten die Rechtfertigung so auf, dass ...'(the Pietists understand justification in such a way that ...')

   i. The first so merely introduces the main clause after the preceding subordinate clause, and here is best left untranslated (cf. Lesson V, note d).
   ii. The second so anticipates the following dass-clause. So frequently has such meanings as 'in this way', 'like this', 'in such a way', 'thus'.

g. durch sich selbst ('through itself')
See Lesson VII, notes d, e.

h. zur Übung seines Gehorsams ('for the exercise of his obedience')
Another example of zu in the sense of 'for the purpose of', see Lesson X, note j.

j. der Christ (hat) alles Kreuz ... zu tragen
For this construction, see Lesson XV, note d.

k. zu Gottes gnädigem Annehmen meiner selbst ('to God's gracious accepting of myself')
Meiner is the gen. of the personal pronoun ich. Such genitives are hardly ever used in modern German speech, but may still be found in literary German. Here is the complete list:

Nom.	Gen.	
ich	meiner	'of me'
du	deiner	'of thee'
er, es	seiner	'of him', 'of it'
sie	ihrer	'of her'
wir	unser	'of us'
ihr	euer	'of you'
sie	ihrer	'of them'
Sie	Ihrer	'of you'

READING PASSAGES

I

Erbarmung, nicht Ungerechtigkeit findet der Mensch bei Gott. Was ist in Gott Barmherzigkeit? In uns entsteht sie durch das Mitleiden, das die Not des anderen mitempfindet und unser Verhalten an sein Leiden anpasst. Die Gemeinschaft des Leidens, die uns aneinander bindet, legt Paulus nicht in Gott hinein. Er verdunkelt, indem er Gottes Barmherzigkeit bezeugt, seine Herrlichkeit nicht. Diese wird gerade darin offenbar, dass er als der Barmherzige alles beseitigt (note a), was uns von ihm trennt, zu uns herantritt und uns so annimmt, wie wir sind, ohne Anspruch an uns, ohne von uns erst eine Leistung zu fordern, die uns seiner würdig machte, in der reinen Güte dessen, der gibt, weil er gütig ist. Darum tut er damit, dass er barmherzig ist (note a), niemand Unrecht. Auch Israel hat ihn nie anders kennengelernt als in der Freiheit seines Erbarmens. Weil er als der Erbarmer an ihm handelt, ward es zum heiligen Volk, empfing es seinen Ruf und erhielt es sein Wort. Sein Erbarmen ist aber sein eigener Wille. Niemand zwingt es ihm ab; er gibt es, wann und wem er will. Das hat Gott auch damals ausgesprochen, als er das Gesetz gab. Durch Mose hat Israel dieselbe göttliche Regel gehört, nach der Gott am Hause Abrahams gehandelt hat. So gilt freilich unser Wille und unsere Bemühung nichts. 9, 16: 'Folglich steht es nicht bei dem, der will, und nicht bei dem, der läuft, sondern bei Gott, der sich erbärmt.' Mein Wollen legt Gott keine Verpflichtung auf; mein Laufen nötigt ihn nicht, mir den Siegespreis zu geben. Was der Mensch will, wie er sich um Gottes Gunst erwirbt, das ist zunächst völlig bedeutungslos; es liegt an Gott selbst, daran, dass er sich erbarmt (note a). Wo haben hier irgend welche Klagen über Gottes Ungerechtigkeit Raum (note b)? Gott hat dem Juden keine Verheissung gebrochen, keine Verpflichtung zerrissen. Er handelt nicht anders, als wie er immer war. Was haben wir daraus zu folgern, wenn wir mit unserem Heil und Leben auf Gott verwiesen sind und er nach seinem eigenen Erbarmen an uns handelt? Dass wir mit Glauben zu ihm aufsehen, mit Bitten uns an ihn wenden, auf seine Barmherzigkeit hoffen und bei ihr anklopfen. Das allein ist die richtige, gerade Folge dazu, dass wir alles, was wir sind, durch Gottes freie Erbarmung sind (note a). Und dann wird es sich zeigen, dass Gott sich in der Tat erbarmt.

(Adolf Schlatter, Der Brief an die Römer. Calwer Verlag, Stuttgart, 1948. in loc.)

II

Paulus weiss (14), welche Bedenken seine Lösung hervorruft. Ungleiche Behandlung bei gleicher Schuld oder Unschuld gilt für Unrecht (ἀδικία). Aber Unrecht ist bei Gott ausgeschlossen. Dass Gott nach freier Willkür sich erbarmt, findet sich Ex. 33,19. Daraus entnimmt Paulus, dass nicht des Menschen Wollen und Rennen, sondern Gottes Erbarmen das Heil gibt (16: ergänze ἡ σωτηρία ἐστίν). Das ist für Paulus, der in seiner Jugend der Gerechtigkeit aus dem Gesetz bis zu völliger Erschöpfung nachgejagt war und sich jetzt vom Messias in seine Gemeinde berufen weiss, überaus tröstlich. Aber er kennt auch Ex. 9, 16, das Wort 'der Schrift' - tatsächlich redet Gott - an Pharao. An Pharao will Gott seine Macht zeigen, damit er Gottes Namen in allen Landteilen verkünde: also die Bestrafung Pharaos dient Gottes Ehre. Aus beiden Bibelstellen zieht aber Paulus (18) den Schluss, dass allein Gottes Wille über Heil und Unheil entscheidet; nach seinem Willen erbarmt er sich des einen und verhärtet den andern. (19) Aber Paulus erwartet nicht bloss den Einwand

They are used particularly after verbs which take the gen. case, e.g. sich erbarmen, 'to have mercy (on)':

Herr, erbarme dich unser!   Lord, have mercy upon us!

In the sentence from the text (above), the verbal noun Annehmen requires a following gen., as in English.

l. das demütige Sichgründen (lit. 'the humble basing oneself'); das Leben-wollen (lit. 'the wanting to live')

   i. Two examples of (practically untranslatable) verbal nouns, formed, like Annehmen in k above, by giving a capital letter to the infinitive and treating it as neuter (cf. Lesson XI, note d.i).

  ii. Note that when reflexive verbs are treated in this way (e.g. sich gründen), they become one word.

 iii. Leben/wollen is an example of a verb whose separable prefix is itself an infinitive. It behaves exactly like a 'normal' separable verb, e.g.

er will allein von Gottes Huld in Christus leben.

Further examples of this type of verb:

kennen/lernen 'to get to know': ich lernte ihn im Jahre 1960 kennen.
fallen/lassen 'to let fall', 'drop' : lass es nicht fallen!
spazieren/gehen 'to go for a walk' : sie sind alle spazierengegan-
gen.

m. es lässt sich nur bezeichnen ... ('it can only be described ...')

See Lesson XI, note e.

Lesson XX

The last lesson of this course provides an opportunity of comparing th
language and the ideas of different authors when they are writing on 1
same theme. Three fairly modern Bible commentators have been chosen:
Adolf Schlatter, Oskar Holtzmann and Karl Barth, and each of them exp
Romans 9:14ff.: 'What shall we say then? Is there unrighteousness wi
God? God forbid ...' The grammatical notes have been kept to a mini

der Ungerechtigkeit, der schon 14 erhoben war, sondern auch, den bestimmten, dass bei solcher Gottesanschauung alle Straffähigkeit des Menschen
wegfalle: τί ἔτι μέμφεται ; Gott kann die Schuld nicht strafen, die er
durch Verstockung herbeiführt. (20) Dem stellt Paulus entgegen, dass das
Geschöpf dem Schöpfer nicht widersprechen, keinen Vorhalt machen darf: das
Gebilde darf sich beim Bildner über seine Gestalt nicht beschweren. Man
fragt sich, ob das recht ist. Der tote Stoff wird sich nicht beklagen,
aber auch der Zögling nicht über seinen Erzieher, der Mann nicht über die
falsche Führung in seinen Jugendjahren? Und 21 vergleicht Paulus die Menschen mit Tongebilden, die der Töpfer je nach Wunsch zur Zier und Unzier
gestalten mag. Dagegen ist zu sagen, dass auch was erst ein vernünftiger
Mensch werden soll, nie bloss ein Spielzeug oder Mittel zum Zweck eines
andern sein darf, sondern dem in ihm angelegten sittlichen Ziele durch
Erziehung und Bildung entgegengeführt werden muss. Auch der werdende
Mensch darf niemals als Ton in des Töpfers Hand frei zu diesen Zwecken
verwendet werden. Es ist also Paulus nicht gelungen, die Bedenken gegen
seine Lösung zu zerstreuen.

(Oskar Holtzmann, Das Neue Testament. Verlag von Alfred Töpelmann in
Giessen, 1926. in loc.)

III

'Ist da nicht eine Unbotmässigkeit auf Seiten Gottes?' 'Den Jakob
liebte ich, Esau aber hasste ich.' Eine furchtbare Wahrheit, um so
furchtbarer, wenn sie uns hier in einer Form entgegentritt, die sich auch
von dem letzten Rest psychologistischer Eindeutigkeit frei hält! Wer ist
der Gott, der s o redet, in dessen Hände zu fallen s o schrecklich ist,
der mit den Seinen (note c) s o umgeht, s o l c h e Not ihnen bereitet?
Der Gott, der so sehr der Gott ist (note d), der Wunder tut, dass er
anders denn im Wunder der Offenbarung, in der Wende von der Verwerfung
zur Erwählung nie und nirgends als Gott erkannt und geglaubt werden kann?
Der Gott, der sich immer finden lässt und gerade darum immer gesucht sein
will? Der Gott, der in alle Ewigkeit der Gott Jakobs ist, und gerade
darum zu jeder Zeit der Gott Esaus? Der Gott, der viel zu sehr (note d)
die Wahrheit selber ist, als dass dieser Mensch in dieser Welt 'Gewissheit' von ihm haben könnte? Wer schauderte hier nicht zurück?(note e):
Est enim praedestinatio Dei vere labyrinthus, unde hominis ingenium nullo
modo se explicare queat (Calvin). Ist es nicht offenkundig, dass dieser
Gedanke, den keine ihres Namens werte Kirche zu denken unterlassen darf,
der Angriff auf die Grundlage jeder Kirche ist? Dass alle unsre religiös-
sittlichen Begrifflichkeiten angesichts der Realität dieses Gottes gegeneinander fallen wie auf die Spitze gestellte Kegel, wie die Häuser und
Bäume auf einem futuristischen Bilde? Sind sie nicht allzu begreiflich,
alle jene Einwendungen, die die religiös-kirchliche Eilfertigkeit und
Kurzatmigkeit zu allen Zeiten im Namen des höchst bedrohten Menschen
gegen die Prädestinationslehre erhoben hat? Ist es nicht unvermeidlich,
dass auch vom höchsten, kühnsten Gipfel menschlichen Glaubens immer und
immer wieder jene tolle Frage (3,5) aufsteigt, ob dieser Gott nicht selber 'unbotmässig' sei: ein launischer, tückischer Dämon, der uns zum
Narren hält, ein Aufrührer gegen die Norm der Gerechtigkeit, der doch
auch e r unterstellt sein müsste? (note f) Gibt es etwas Empörenderes
für den Menschen als das majestätische Geheimnis dieses Unerforschlichen,
Unzugänglichen, Unberührbaren, dieses allein Freien und selbst Mächtigen?

(Karl Barth, Der Römerbrief. Chr. Kaiser Verlag, München, 1933. in loc.)

GRAMMATICAL NOTES

a. Diese wird gerade dárin offenbar, dass er ... alles beseitigt ....

'This becomes manifest precisely in the fact that he puts aside every-thing ...'

Darum tut er dámit, dass er barmherzig ist, niemand Unrecht

'Therefore, by being merciful, he does no-one an injustice'

Es liegt an Gott selbst, dáran, dass er sich erbarmt

'It depends on God himself, on his having mercy'

Das ... ist die ... Folge dázu, dass wir alles .... durch Gottes freie Erbarmung sind

'This is the consequence of the fact that we are everything ... through God's free mercy'

Note this use of da(r)-+ preposition, to anticipate a dass clause. The English translations of this construction will depend on conside-rations of style, but initially the meaning can usually be arrived at by the use of the formula '... the fact that ...'

b. Wo haben hier irgend welche Klagen über Gottes Ungerechtigkeit Raum? (lit. 'Where do any complaints at all about God's injustice have (any) place?')

Welcher, etc. (usual meaning:'which') sometimes means 'any' or 'some'.

c. mit den Seinen ('with his people')

This use of the possessive adjective as a noun is quite common. Any of the possessive adjectives can be used, e.g. die Meinen 'my people'. Luther renders John 1,11 thus: 'Er kam in sein Eigentum (=property), und die Seinen nahmen ihn nicht auf.'

d. der Gott, der so sehr der Gott ist ... '... so much ...'

der Gott, der viel zu sehr die Wahrheit selber ist ... '... too much ...'

Sehr (usual meaning: 'very') is also used adverbially in the sense of '(very) much', e.g.

Ich liebe ihn sehr.

e. Wer schauderte hier nicht zurück? ('Who would not shrink back at this?')

Schauderte is imperfect subjunctive. Being a weak verb, it has imperfect subjunctive identical with imperfect indicative (see Lesson X, Introduc-tion 2.i.).

f. Gerechtigkeit, der doch auch e r unterstellt sein müsste ('justice, to which after all he too ought to be subject')

The following imperfect subjunctives will be found, all translatable by English 'ought': müsste, sollte, dürfte

The nuances of meaning which distinguish them are very fine indeed, and cannot be expressed in English without a great deal of paraphrasing. Similarly, all three verbs are used to express 'ought to have ...', e.g. Er hätte gehen müssen/sollen/dürfen, 'He ought to have gone'.

Appendix I
German Grammatical Tables

1. <u>DEFINITE ARTICLE</u> (=the)

	Masculine	Feminine	Neuter	Plural
Nominative	der	die	das	die
Accusative	den	die	das	die
Genitive	des --(e)s	der	des --(e)s	der
Dative	dem	der	dem	den --n

The following words take the same endings as the definite article:

dieser = this
jener = that
jeder = each
welcher = which

2. <u>INDEFINITE ARTICLE</u> (=a, an)

	Masculine	Feminine	Neuter	
Nominative	ein	eine	ein	
Accusative	einen	eine	ein	NO
Genitive	eines --(e)s	einer	eines --(e)s	PLURAL
Dative	einem	einer	einem	

The following words take the same endings as the indefinite article:

kein = not a, not any   ihr = her, their
mein = my   unser = our
dein = your (fam. sing.)   euer = your (fam. pl.)
sein = his, its   Ihr = your (polite)

If these words are followed by a <u>plural</u> noun, e.g. my <u>books</u>, they take the endings of the plural <u>definite</u> article (see 1. above): meine Bücher.

3. <u>CASES OF PRONOUNS</u>

		Nominative	Accusative	Dative
Singular	1.	ich	mich	mir
	2.	du	dich	dir
	3.	er	ihn	ihm
		sie	sie	ihr
		es	es	ihm

Plural				
	1.	wir	uns	uns
	2.	ihr	euch	euch
	3.	sie	sie	ihnen
		Sie	Sie	Ihnen

Reflexive pronouns (acc. and dat.) are identical with the above, except that all the 3rd person pronouns, both singular and plural, are replaced by 'sich': e.g. er reformierte sich, sie reformierten sich.

4. TENSES OF VERBS

(For a list of all strong and irregular weak verbs used in the course, see 5. below)

WEAK	STRONG
MACH EN	NEHM EN

PRESENT:

	WEAK			STRONG	
ich mach	E = I make, am making, etc.		ich nehm	E = I take, am taking, etc.	
du mach	ST		du NIMM	ST	
er, sie, es mach	T		er, sie, es NIMM	T	
wir mach	EN		wir nehm	EN	
ihr mach	T		ihr nehm	T	
sie, Sie mach	EN		sie, Sie nehm	EN	

IMPERFECT:

	WEAK		STRONG	
ich mach	TE = I made, was making, etc.	ich NAHM	= I took, was taking, etc.	
du mach	TEST	du NAHM	ST	
er, sie, es mach	TE	er, sie, es NAHM		
wir mach	TEN	wir NAHM	EN	
ihr mach	TET	ihr NAHM	T	
sie, Sie mach	TEN	sie, Sie NAHM	EN	

PERFECT:

ich habe GE/mach/T = I have made, have been making, etc.

ich habe GE/NOMM/EN = I have taken, have been taking, etc.

PLUPERFECT:

ich hatte gemacht = I had made, had been making, etc.

ich hatte genommen = I had taken, had been taking, etc.

FUTURE:

ich werde MACHEN = I shall make, shall be making, etc.

ich werde NEHMEN = I shall take, shall be taking, etc.

Separable verbs insert 'ge' between prefix and stem in past participle:
e.g. vor/stellen (to introduce): ich habe vorgestellt.

Inseparable and -ieren verbs have no 'ge' in past participle:
e.g. bestellen (to order): ich habe bestellt
telefonieren (to telephone): ich habe telefoniert.

Intransitive verbs denoting a change of place or state form their perfect tenses with sein, not haben:

e.g. kommen (to come): ich bin gekommen (perfect)
werden (to become): ich war geworden (pluperfect).

5. <u>STRONG (and irregular weak) VERBS OCCURRING IN THE COURSE</u>

N.B. (a) only 3rd person sing. is given, unless otherwise indicated;
    (b) sep. or insep. verbs are not given as such - only the simple
        verb is given;
    (c) a dash (-) indicates the form is regular.

INFINITIVE	PRESENT	IMPERFECT	PERFECT
beginnen (begin)	-	begann	hat begonnen
bergen (conceal; salvage)	birgt	barg	hat geborgen
bieten (offer)	-	bot	hat geboten
binden (tie)	-	band	hat gebunden
bitten (ask)	-	bat	hat gebeten
bleiben (stay)	-	blieb	ist geblieben
brechen (break)	bricht	brach	hat gebrochen
bringen (bring)	-	brachte	hat gebracht
denken (think)	-	dachte	hat gedacht
dürfen (be allowed)	ich, er darf, du darfst	durfte	hat gedurft
essen (eat)	du, er isst	ass	hat gegessen
fahren (travel)	fährt	fuhr	ist gefahren
fallen (fall)	fällt	fiel	ist gefallen
fangen (catch)	fängt	fing	hat gefangen
finden (find)	-	fand	hat gefunden
gebären (bear)	gebiert	gebar	hat geboren
geben (give)	gibt	gab	hat gegeben
gehen (go)	-	ging	ist gegangen
gelingen (succeed)	-	gelang	ist gelungen
gelten (be valid, appl.)	gilt	galt	hat gegolten
geschehen (happen)	geschieht	geschah	ist geschehen
gewinnen (win)	-	gewann	hat gewonnen
gleichen (equal)	-	glich	hat geglichen
graben (bury)	gräbt	grub	hat gegraben
greifen (seize)	-	griff	hat gegriffen
haben (have)	hat	hatte	hat gehabt
halten (hold)	du hältst, er hält	hielt	hat gehalten
hängen (hang)	-	hing	hat gehangen
heben (raise)	-	hob	hat gehoben
heissen (be called)	-	hiess	hat geheissen
kennen (know)	-	kannte	hat gekannt
kommen (come)	-	kam	ist gekommen
können (be able)	ich, er kann, du kannst	konnte	hat gekonnt
lassen (let)	du, er lässt	liess	hat gelassen
laufen (run)	läuft	lief	ist gelaufen
leiden (suffer)	-	litt	hat gelitten
lesen (read)	du, er liest	las	hat gelesen
liegen (lie)	-	lag	hat gelegen
mögen (like)	ich, er mag, du magst	mochte	hat gemocht
müssen (have to)	ich, er muss, du musst	musste	hat gemusst
nehmen (take)	nimmt	nahm	hat genommen
nennen (name)	-	nannte	hat genannt
raten (advise)	du rätst, er rät	riet	hat geraten
reissen (tear)	-	riss	hat gerissen
rennen (race, run)	-	rannte	ist gerannt
rufen (call)	-	rief	hat gerufen
saufen (drink)	sauft	soff	hat gesoffen
schaffen (create)	-	schuf	hat geschaffen
scheiden (separate)	-	schied	hat geschieden

Grammatical Tables

INFINITIVE	PRESENT	IMPERFECT	PERFECT
scheinen (seem; shine)	–	schien	hat geschienen
schliessen (shut)	–	schloss	hat geschlossen
schlingen (swallow)	–	schlang	hat geschlungen
schneiden (cut)	–	schnitt	hat geschnitten
schreiben (write)	–	schrieb	hat geschrieben
schreien (cry, shout)	–	schrie	hat geschrieen
sehen (see)	sieht	sah	hat gesehen
sein (be)	ich bin, du bist, er ist	war	ist gewesen
	wir, sie sind, ihr seid		
senden (send)	–	sandte	hat gesandt
singen (sing)	–	sang	hat gesungen
sitzen (sit)	du, er sitzt	sass	hat gesessen
sollen (be supposed to)			
	ich, er soll, du sollst	sollte	hat gesollt
sprechen (speak)	spricht	sprach	hat gesprochen
stehen (stand)	–	stand	hat gestanden
stehlen (steal)	stiehlt	stahl	hat gestohlen
steigen (climb)	–	stieg	ist gestiegen
sterben (die)	stirbt	starb	ist gestorben
stossen (push, thrust)	stösst	stiess	hat gestossen
tragen (carry)	trägt	trug	hat getragen
treffen (meet)	trifft	traf	hat getroffen
treten (step)	du trittst, er tritt	trat	ist getreten
tun (do)	du tust, er tut	tat	hat getan
verlieren (lose)	–	verlór	hat verlóren
wachsen (grow)	du, er wächst	wuchs	ist gewachsen
weisen (point)	–	wies	hat gewiesen
wenden (turn)	–	wandte	hat gewandt
werben (woo)	wirbt	warb	hat geworben
werden (become)	du wirst, er wird	wurde	ist geworden
werfen (throw)	wirft	warf	hat geworfen
wiegen (weigh)	–	wog	hat gewogen
winden (wind)	–	wand	hat gewunden
wissen (know)	ich, er weiss, du weisst	wusste	hat gewusst
wollen (want)	ich, er will, du willst	wollte	hat gewollt
ziehen (pull)	–	zog	hat gezogen

Appendix II
Books of the Bible

1. <u>OLD TESTAMENT</u> (Das Alte Testament) (A.T.)

Das erste Buch Mose	(1.Mose)	Genesis
Das zweite Buch Mose	(2.Mose)	Exodus
Das dritte Buch Mose	(3.Mose)	Leviticus
Das vierte Buch Mose	(4.Mose)	Numbers
Das fünfte Buch Mose	(5.Mose)	Deuteronomy
Das Buch Josua	(Jos.)	Joshua
Das Buch der Richter	(Richt.)	Judges
Das Buch Ruth	(Ruth)	Ruth
Das erste Buch Samuélis	(1.Sam.)	1 Samuel
Das zweite Buch Samuélis	(2.Sam.)	2 Samuel
Das erste Buch von den Königen	(1.Kön.)	1 Kings
Das zweite Buch von den Königen	(2.Kön.)	2 Kings
Das erste Buch der Chronika	(1.Chron.)	1 Chronicles
Das zweite Buch der Chronika	(2.Chron.)	2 Chronicles
Das Buch Esra	(Esr.)	Ezra
Das Buch Nehemia	(Neh.)	Nehemiah
Das Buch Esther	(Esth.)	Esther
Das Buch Hiob	(Hiob)	Job
Der Psalter (or: die Psalmen)	(Ps.)	Psalms
Die Sprüche Salomos	(Spr.)	Proverbs
Der Prediger Salomo	(Pred.)	Ecclesiastes
Das Hohelied Salomos	(Hohel.)	Song of Solomon
Jesája	(Jes.)	Isaiah
Jeremía	(Jer.)	Jeremiah
Die Klag(e)lieder Jeremias	(Klagl.)	Lamentations
Hesékiel	(Hesek.)	Ezekiel
Daniel	(Dan.)	Daniel
Hosea	(Hos.)	Hosea
Joel	(Joel)	Joel
Amos	(Amos)	Amos
Obádja	(Obad.)	Obadiah
Jona	(Jon.)	Jonah
Micha	(Mich.)	Micah
Nahum	(Nah.)	Nahum
Habakuk	(Hab.)	Habakkuk
Zephánja	(Zeph.)	Zephaniah
Haggai	(Hagg.)	Haggai
Sachárja	(Sach.)	Zechariah
Maleáchi	(Mal.)	Malachi

2. <u>APOCRYPHA</u> (Die Apokrýphen)

Das Buch Judith	Judith
Die Weisheit Salomos	Wisdom

Das Buch Tobit	Tobit
Die Sprüche Jesus', des Sohnes Sirachs	Ecclesiasticus
Die Sprüche Baruch	Baruch
Die erste Buch der Makkabäer	1 Maccabees
Das zweite Buch der Makkabäer	2 Maccabees
Zusätze zum Buch Esther	The rest of Esther
Zusätze zum Buch Daniel	The rest of Daniel

3. <u>NEW TESTAMENT (Das Neue Testament) (N.T.)</u>

Das Evangelium des Matthäus	(Matth.)	(Mt.)	Matthew
Das Evangelium des Markus	(Mark.)		Mark
Das Evangelium des Lukas	(Luk.)		Luke
Das Evangelium des Johannes	(Joh.)		John
Die Apostelgeschichte des Lukas	(Apg.)		Acts
Der Brief des Paulus an die Römer			
(or: Der Römerbrief)	(Röm.)		Romans
Der erste Brief des Paulus an die Korinther			
(or: Der erste Korintherbrief)	(1.Kor.)		1 Corinthians
Der zweite Brief des Paulus an die Korinther			
(or: Der zweite Korintherbrief)	(2.Kor.)		2 Corinthians
Der Brief des Paulus an die Galáter			
(or: Der Galáterbrief)	(Gal.)		Galatians

(likewise for the remaining Pauline Epistles; only the short form is indicated here):

Der Epheserbrief	(Eph.)	Ephesians
Der Philipperbrief	(Phil.)	Philippians
Der Kolosserbrief	(Kol.)	Colossians
Der erste Thessalonicherbrief	(1.Thess.)	1 Thessalonians
Der zweite Thessalonicherbrief	(2.Thess.)	2 Thessalonians
Der erste Timotheusbrief	(1.Tim.)	1 Timothy
Der zweite Timotheusbrief	(2.Tim.)	2 Timothy
Der Titusbrief	(Tit.)	Titus
Der Philemonbrief	(Philem.)	Philemon
Der erste Brief des Petrus	(1.Petr.)	1 Peter
Der zweite Brief des Petrus	(2.Petr.)	2 Peter
Der erste Brief des Johannes	(1.Joh.)	1 John
Der zweite Brief des Johannes	(2.Joh.)	2 John
Der dritte Brief des Johannes	(3.Joh.)	3 John
Der Brief an die Hebräer		
(or: Der Hebräerbrief)	(Hebr.)	Hebrews

(the older form Ebräer (Ebr.) is sometimes found)

Der Brief des Jakóbus	(Jak.)	James
Der Brief des Judas	(Judä.)	Jude
Die Offenbárung des Johannes	(Offenb.)	Revelation

Vocabulary

Not all the irregular parts of strong verbs are included here, but only those which occur in the course. In the case of separable verbs, only the strong parts of the simple verb are given, e.g. aussprechen (pres. <u>spricht</u>). Compound nouns are not normally given as such when their meaning can be ascertained from their component parts, e.g. Weltrichter, Menschensohn. Where stress is not indicated ($'$) it can be assumed to fall on the first syllable.

<u>Abbreviations</u>:

acc.	accusative	gen.	genitive	prep.	preposition
adj.	adjective	imp.	imperfect	pres.	present
adv.	adverb	insep.	inseparable	sep.	separable
conj.	conjunction	pl.	plural	sing.	singular
dat.	dative	p.p.	past participle		

A

ab (see von ... ab)
das Abbild(er) image, copy
der Abend(e) evening
aber but, however
die Abhandlung(en) treatise, discourse
der Ablauf course
áb/legen (sep.) (see Zeugnis)
áb/lehnen (sep.) to refuse, turn down
áb/leiten (sep.) to deduce
die Absage refusal; renunciation
der Abschluss conclusion, end
der Abschnitt(e) extract
absolviéren to complete (studies)
áb/tun (sep.)(p.p. <u>getan</u>) to abolish, do away with
áb/weichen (sep.) to diverge, deviate
die Abzweckung(en) aim, purpose, intent
áb/zwingen (sep.)(+<u>dat</u>.) to force from
ach! oh!
der Acker(Ä) field, arable land
Ägýpten Egypt
ägýptisch Egyptian
ähnlich (+<u>dat</u>.) similar
alléin (adv.) alone; (conj.) but, only

állerdings it's true; to be sure
alles all, everything
allgeméin general
der Allherscher(-) sovereign
die Allmacht omnipotence
der Allmächtige the Almighty
allzu too
als as; when; than
also (adv.) so; (conj.) therefore
alt old
das Alter(-) age
der Alttestaméntler O.T. scholar
alttestaméntlich O.T. (adj.)
an (+<u>acc</u>.) up to, to; (+<u>dat</u>.) at, on
án/beten (sep.) to worship, adore
ander other
ändern to alter, change
anders als (<u>or</u> denn) otherwise than
die Änderung(en) álteration, change
aneinánder to one another
der Anfang(ä/e) beginning
die Anfechtung(en) temptation; spiritual conflict
án/fertigen (sep.) to make, produce

die Anfertigung production, making

die Anforderung(en) demand

Anforderung stellen an (+acc.) to make demands on

angesichts (+gen.) in the face of

die Angleichung an (+acc.) matching up, adaptation, adjustment to

der Angriff(e) attack

die Angst fear

an/klagen (sep.) to accuse

an/klopfen (sep.) bei (+dat.) to knock at the door of

der Anlass(ä/e) occasion, rise, cause

Anlass geben zu (+dat.) to give occasion for

an/legen (sep.) to implant

die Anleitung guidance

an/muten (sep.) to give the impression of, have a feeling of

annehmbar acceptable

an/nehmen (sep.)(pres. nimmt) to accept

an/passen (sep.) an (+acc.) to adapt to, suit to

die Anpassung an (+acc.) adaptation, matching up, accommodation to

an/rücken (sep.) to advance

an/schauen (sep.) to view, look at

die Anschauung(en) view, outlook

sich an/schliessen (sep.)(+dat.) or an (+acc.) to join, follow on

an/sehen (sep.) to look at

ansehen als to regard as

an/sprechen (sep.) to speak to

ansprechen als to regard as

der Anspruch(ü/e) claim

ohne Anspruch an (+acc.) without making any demands on

der Anteil(e) part, share

Anteil haben/gewinnen an (+dat.) to have/gain a part in

die Antwort(en) answer

antworten to answer

die Anweisung(en) instruction, guidance

der Apostel(-) apostle

die Apostelgeschichte Acts of the Apostles

der Apparát(e) apparatus; material

die Arbeit(en) work

arbeiten to work

arm poor

die Armut poverty

die Art(en) kind, sort; manner

auch also; even

auf (+acc.) on(to); (+dat.) on

auf (+acc.) ... hin in response to, on the strength of

auf/erstehen (sep.) to rise (from dead)

die Auferstehung resurrection

auf/erwecken (sep.) to raise (from dead)

auf/fassen (sep.) to understand, conceive

die Aufgabe(n) task; exercise

die Aufhebung abrogation, repeal

unter Aufhebung von (+dat.) by abolishing, by getting rid of

auf/hören (sep.) to cease

die Auflage(n) edition

auf/legen (sep.) to impose

auf/leuchten (sep.) to blaze forth, shine out

aufmerksam auf (+acc.) attentive to

die Aufmerksamkeit attention, attentiveness

auf/richten (sep.) to set up, establish

der Aufrührer(-) rebel

der Aufsatz(ä/e) essay

auf/sehen (sep.) to look up

auf/steigen (sep.) to crop up, arise

der Auftrag(ä/e) task, mandate; order

auf/tun (sep.) to open

das Auge(n) eye

aus (+dat.) out of, from

der Ausgang(ä/e) exit, way out

der Ausgangspunkt(e) point of departure

aus/gehen (sep.) von (+dat.) to go out from; proceed from

aus/richten (sep.) to execute, carry out

eine Botschaft áusrichten
   to deliver a message
áus/schliessen (sep.)(p.p.
   geschlossen) to exclude;
   (p.p.) out of the question
aussen outside
   nach aussen (to the) outside, outwards
ausserhalb (+gen.) outside
äussern to utter
äusserst extremely
áus/speien (sep.) to spit out
áus/sprechen (sep.)(pres.
   spricht; p.p. gesprochen)
   to pronounce; express;
   state
áus/stossen (sep.)(p.p. gestoss-
   en) to thrust out, expel
áus/ziehen (sep.)(imp. zog;
   p.p. gezogen) to move
   out, go out
die Autoritä̈t authority

                    B

bald soon
der Band(ä/e) volume
barmhérzig merciful
die Barmhérzigkeit mercy
der Bauch(äu/e) belly
bauen to build
der Bauer(n) peasant; farmer
   bäuerlich rural
'der Baum(äu/e) tree
das Bedénken misgivings
bedéuten (insep.) to mean
bedéutsam meaningful,
   significant
die Bedéutung(en) meaning
bedéutungslos meaningless
die Bedíngung(en) condition;
   requisite
bedíngungslos unconditional
bedróhen (insep.) to
   threaten
das Bedúrfnis(se) need, neces-
   sity
beéinflussen (insep.) to influence
beéinträchtigen to infringe,
   encroach on
beféstigen (insep.) to for-
   tify
befréien (insep.) to free,
   liberate

begéistert enthusiastic-
   (ally)
begínnen (insep.)(imp. begánn;
   p.p. begónnen) to begin
begráben (insep.)(p.p. begráben) to bury
begréifen (insep.) to understand, grasp
begréiflich comprehensible,
   understandable
der Begríff(e) idea, concept
die Begrífflichkeit concept,
   conception
begründen (insep.) to ex-
   plain, give reasons for
sich begründen to arise
behándeln (insep.)(pres. ich
   behándle) to treat,
   deal with
die Behándlung treatment,
   dealing
behérbergen (insep.) to
   shelter, take in
bei (+dat.) with; at the
   house of; while, in the
   writings of; in the case
   of
béi/bringen (+dat.)(sep.)(p.p.
   gebracht) to teach
beide both
bei/legen (sep.) to attri-
   bute, ascribe
das Beispiel(e) example
   zum Beispiel (z.B.) for
   example, e.g.
der Beistand assistance; coun-
   sel, advocate
bekánnt (well)known
bekánntlich as is well
   known
bekéhren (insep.) to convert
sich bekéhren to be converted
die Bekéhrung(en) conversion
bekénnen (insep.) to confess;
   profess
das Bekénntnis(se) confession,
   profession; denomination
sich beklágen (insep.) to complain
bekléiden (insep.) to clothe
belánglos unimportant, of no
   consequence
belásten (insep.) to weigh
   down, burden
der Belég(e) proof, evidence
bemérken (insep.) to notice;
   remark

Vocabulary

die Bemérkung(en)   remark
die Bemühung(en)   exertion
    beóbachten (insep.)   to ob-
        serve, watch
die Beóbachtung(en)   observation
    beréiten (insep.)   to prepare;
        cause, give
    beréits   already
der Berg(e)   mountain
der Bergmann (pl. Bergleute)
        miner
    berúfen (insep.)(p.p. berúfen)
        to call
    berühren (insep.)   to touch
sich berühren mit (+dat.)   to be
        in harmony with
    beschnéiden (insep.)   to
        circumcise
die Beschnéidung   circumcision
    beschréiben (insep.)(p.p.
        beschríeben)   to
        descríbe
sich beschwéren (insep.)   to com-
        plain
    beséitigen (insep.)   to
        remove, put aside
    besítzen (insep.)(imp.
        besass)   to possess
    besónder(s)   especial(ly)
    bespréngen (insep.)   to
        sprinkle
    bestéhen (insep.) aus (+dat.)
        (imp. bestánd)   to con-
        sist of
    bestéllen (insep.)   to order;
        till, cultivate
    bestímmen (insep.) zu (+dat.)
        to destine for
    bestímmt   definite(ly),
        precise(ly)
die Bestráfung(en)   punishment
    besúchen (insep.)   to visit
    beten   to pray
    betónen (insep.)   to emphasize,
        stress
die Betónung   emphasis, stress
    betráchten (insep.)   to consi-
        der
    betréffen (insep.)   to con-
        cern, affect
    was (+acc.) betrífft   as far
        as ... is concerned
    bewáhren (insep.) vor (+dat.)
        to keep, preserve from
die Bewégung(en)   movement;
        emotion

der Bewéis(e)   proof
    bewóhnen (insep.)   to inhabit
der Bewóhner(-)   inhabitant,
        dweller
die Bewúnderung   admiration
    bezéichnen (insep.)   to term;
        indicate; characterize
die Bezéichnung(en)   designation
    bezéugen (insep.)   to testify
        to
die Bezéugung   testimony; testi-
        fying
    bezíehen   to enter (univer-
        sity, etc.)
die Bezíehung(en)   respect,
        reference, relation
    in irgend einer Bezíehung
    in any respect
die Bibel(n)   Bible
    biblisch   biblical
das Bild(er)   picture, image
    bilden   to form
der Bildner(-)   sculptor
die Bildung   culture, education
    ich bin   I am
    binden   to bind, tie; to be
        binding on
    bis zu (+dat.)   until, as
        far as, up to
    bishér   hitherto
    bishérig   hitherto existing
    du bist   thou art
die Bitte(n)   request
    bleiben (imp. blieb; p.p.
        geblíeben)   to remain,
        stay
    bloss   mere(ly), only
das Blut   blood
der Boden   soil, ground
    böse   wicked, evil; angry
die Botschaft(en)   message
    brauchen   to need; use
    brechen (p.p. gebrochen)   to
        break
der Brief(e)   letter, epistle
    bringen (imp. brachte)   to
        bring, take
das Brot(e)   bread; loaf
der Bruch(ü/e)   break, rupture
der Bruder(ü)   brother
das Buch(ü/er)   book
der Búchstabe(gen. -ns;   all
        other cases -n)
        letter (of alphabet)
der Bund(ü/e)   covenant; federa-
        tion

die Busse   repentance; penance
  Busse tun   to repent; do
    penance

C

der Christ (all other cases -en)
    Christian
die Christenheit   Christendom
  christlich   Christian
  Christus (gen. Christi; dat.
    Christo)   Christ

D

da (conj.)   as, since; (adv.)
    there
dagégen   on the other hand
dahér (or dáher)   therefore,
    hence
dámalig   of that time
dámals   at that time
damít (adv.)   with it; (conj.)
    in order that
dámit   with this, thereby
    (see Lesson XX, note a)
dann   then
darán   (see Lesson XX, note a)
daráuf   (see Lesson XX, note a)
daraufhín   in view of this, so
daráus   (see Lesson XX, note a)
dár/bringen (sep.)   to bring
    (a sacrifice, etc.)
darf (1st and 3rd sing. pres. of
    dürfen)   'may'
darín   (see Lesson XX, note a)
dár/stellen (sep.)   to repres-
    ent, make a representation
    of, present
die Dárstellung(en)   presentation
    (of facts, etc.)
darúm   therefore
das (pronoun)   that, this;
    (article, neuter)   the
dass (conj.)   that
die Dauer   duration
  auf die Dauer   in the long
    run
  dauern   to last
  dazú   in addition
  dázu   (see Lesson XX, note a)
die Debátte(n)   debate
  debattíerbar   debatable
  debattíeren   to debate

dein   thy
démgemáss   according to this
démnach   accordingly
die Demut   humility, meekness
  démütig   humble, meek
  denken (p.p. gedacht) an
    (+acc.)   to think (of)
  denn (conj.)   for; (particle)
    then
der/gléiche (both parts de-
    cline)   the same
der/jénige (both parts de-
    cline)   (see Lesson XIX,
    note a)
der/sélbe (both parts decline)
    the same (see Lesson XIX,
    note a)
déshalb   therefore, thus,
    for that reason
déswegen   because of that,
    for that reason
deutlich   clear(ly), dis-
    tinct(ly)
deutsch   German (adj. and
    the German language)
der Deutsche (declines as adjec-
    tive)   German (man)
  Deutschland   Germany
  dich (acc. of du)   thee
  dienen (+dat.)   to serve
  dieser (declines like defi-
    nite article)   this;
    that
  dies ist   this is
das Ding(e)   thing
  dir (dat. of du)   (to) thee
  doch   yet, after all
  drei   three
  dringen   to urge
  dringend   urgent
  dritt   third
  du   thou
  durch (+acc.)   through; by
    means of
  durcháus nicht   by no means
der Durchbruch   breakthrough
  durcheinánder/werfen (sep.)
    (p.p. geworfen)   to
    confuse, mix up
  dürfen (pres. darf; imp.
    durfte)   to be allowed
    to, 'may' (see Lesson
    XIII, note c)
  durstig   thirsty

E

eben (adj.) level, even;
(adv.) precisely; just,
simply

eben damit for that very
reason

ebensowenig just a little;
likewise (in a negative
context)

die Ehre honour

eigen own

eigentlich actual(ly),
real(ly)

eigentümlich peculiar

die Eigentümlichkeit peculiarity

die Eilfertigkeit hastiness,
overhaste

die Eindeutigkeit unequivocal-
ness, unambiguity

der Eindruck(ü/e) impression

eindrucksvoll impressive

ein, eine (indefinite article)
a, an

einfach simple

die Einfachheit simplicity

der Einfluss(ü/e) influence

ein/gehen (sep.) auf (or in)
(+acc.) to go into,
enter into

die Einheit unity; unit

einige some, few

die Einleitung(en) introduction

ein/leuchten (sep.) to
illumine

ein/nehmen (sep.) to occupy

eins one

ein/schliessen (sep.) to
include

einseitig one-sided(ly)

ein/setzen (sep.) to appoint,
install

einsichtig (+dat.) intelligible, intelligent

ein/treten/(sep.) in (+acc.)
(imp. trat) to enter,
go into

der Einwand(ä/e) objection

die Einwendung(en) objection

die Einzelheit(en) detail

einzeln individual; one or
two

die Eltern (pl. only) parents

empfangen (insep.)(pres.
empfängt; imp. empfing;
p.p. empfangen) to

receive; conceive (a
child)

die Empfängnis conception

die unbefleckte Empfängnis
immaculate conception

die Empfängnisverhütung contra-
ception

empfinden (insep.)(imp.
empfand) to feel; be
sensible of

empörend revolting, shock-
ing

das Ende(n) end

enden to end

endlich finally, at last

der Engel(-) angel

entdecken (insep.) to
discover

die Entdeckung(en) discovery

entfallen (insep.) auf
(+acc.) to fall to
someone's share, be
apportioned to

entfalten (insep.) to
unfold

entgegen/führen (sep.)
(+dat.) to lead
towards

entgegen/setzen (sep.)(+dat.)
to set over against

entgegen/stellen (sep.)
(+dat.) to set
against, oppose

entgegen/treten (sep.)
(+dat.) to come to
meet; to meet, encoun-
ter

enthalten (insep.)(pres.
enthält) to contain

entnehmen (insep.) aus
(+dat.)(p.p. ent-
nimmt) to deduce
from

entscheiden (imp. entschied;
p.p. entschieden) to
decide; to be decisive

auf entschiedenste most
decidedly

die Entscheidung(en) decision;
decree

sich entschliessen (insep.) to
decide, make up one's
mind

der Entschluss(ü/e) decision

entsprechen (insep.)(+dat.)
to correspond to

entstéhen (insep.) to arise, come into being
die Entstéhung origin, genesis
entwéihen (insep.) to desecrate, profane
die Entwícklung(en) development
das Epítheton (pl. Epítheta) epithet
er he; it (referring to masc. noun)
das Eráchten opinion, judgment
meines Eráchtens in my opinion
das Erbármen pity, compassion
sich erbármen (insep.)(+gen.) to have mercy on
der Erbármer(-) one who has mercy
die Erbármung mercy, pity
erbáuen (insep.) to edify, build up
erbáulich edifying
das Erbe inheritance
erben to inherit
die Erbsünde original sin
die Erde earth
sich eréignen (insep.) to occur
das Eréignis(se) event, occurrence
der Eremít(en) hermit, anchorite
erfáhren (insep.) to experience; learn
die Erfáhrung(en) experience
erfássen (insep.) als to conceive as
erfínden (insep.) to invent
die Erfíndung(en) invention; device(s)
erfórderlich requisite, necessary
erfórschen (insep.) to investigate, discover by research
erfüllen (insep.) to fulfil, fill
die Erfüllung(en) fulfilment
ergánzen to complete
ergánze 'supply the words'
sich ergében (insep.)(pres. ergíbt) to submit, resign oneself; to result
ergében (+dat.) submissive, devoted to
die Ergébenheit submissiveness, devotion
das Ergébnis(se) result
ergéhen (insep.)(p.p. ergángen)

to be issued (of laws, etc.)
erhálten (insep.)(imp. erhíelt) to maintain; to keep, retain; to receive
erhében (insep.)(p.p. erhóben) to raise
erhóffen (insep.) to hope for
sich erínnern (insep.) an (+acc.) to remember
erkénnen (insep.)(p.p. erkánnt) to recognize; to know personally
die Erkénntnis recognition; personal knowledge
erklären (insep.) to explain; to declare, state
erlángen (insep.) to attain
erlösen (insep.) to redeem
der Erlöser(-) redeemer
die Erlösung salvation, redemption
ernéuen (insep.) to renew
ernst serious, grave, earnest
der Ernst seriousness, gravity, earnestness
eröffnen (insep.) to open, open up
errétten (insep.) to save, deliver
der Errétter(-) deliverer
die Erréttung deliverance
ersaufen (insep.)(p.p. ersoffen) to drown (intrans.)
erschéinen (insep.)(p.p. erschíenen) to appear
die Erschöpfung exhaustion
erschrécken (insep.) to frighten
ersétzen (insep.) to replace, substitute
erst (adj.) first; (adv.) first; not until, only; some day (in the future)
erstícken (insep.) to suffocate, stifle
die Erwählung election
erwárten (insep.) to expect
die Erwártung(en) expectation
erwécken (insep.) to awaken, rouse
die Erwéckung(en) awakening;

revival

der Erwéis(e) proof, demon-
    stration

sich erwéisen (insep.) to
    prove oneself, show
    oneself

erwérben (insep.)(p.p. erwórben)
    to gain, acquire

sich erwérben (insep.)(pres. erwírbt)
    um (+acc.) to seek to
    obtain

erzählen (insep.) to tell,
    relate, recount

der Erziéher(-) educator

die Erziéhung education

es it

essen (p.p. gegéssen) to eat

etwa approximately; for
    example

etwas something; somewhat,
    to some extent; some

euch (acc. and dat. of ihr)
    (to) you

euer your
    um euretwillen for your
    sakes

evangélisch Protestant, esp.
    Lutheran; of the Gospel,
    evangelical

das Evangélium (pl. Evangélien)
    Gospel

ewig eternal

die Éwigkeit eternity
    in alle Éwigkeit to (all)
    eternity

F

die Fähigkeit(en) capacity, capa-
    bility

fahren (pres. fährt) to go,
    travel

die Fakultät(en) (university)
    faculty

der Fall(ä/e) case, event

fallen to fall

fällen to fell; to pass
    (law, etc.)

falsch wrong; false

fassbar tangible, palpable;
    intelligible

fassen to seize; to enclose;
    to conceive, understand

fast almost

fehlen to be missing, be
    absent

der Feind(e) enemy

das Feld(er) field

fest firm(ly)

die Féstgabe festive gift,
    presentation

fést/stehen (sep.) to be
    firmly established,
    be beyond question

fést/stellen (sep.) to
    ascertain, establish,
    find out

finden (imp. fand; p.p. ge-
    funden) to find

sich finden to be found

finster dark, gloomy

die Finsternis darkness

der Fisch(e) fish

das Fleisch flesh, meat

fleischern fleshly; carnal

der Fleiss diligence

fleissig diligent

der Fluch(ü/e) curse

die Flut(en) flood; high tide

die Folge(n) consequence

folgen (+dat.) to follow

folgern aus (+dat.) to
    conclude from

folglich consequent(ly)

fordern to demand, require

die Formel(n) formula

fórt/setzen (sep.) to con-
    tinue

die Frage(n) question

fragen to ask

sich fragen to ask oneself,
    wonder

die Frau(en) woman; wife; Mrs

frei free(ly)

die Freiheit freedom

freilich of course,
    certainly

fremd strange, unfamiliar;
    foreign

die Freude(n) joy

der Frevel misdeed, wicked act

frevelhaft wicked, out-
    rageous

der Friede (gen. -ns; all other
    cases -n) peace

fröhlich merry, cheerful

fromm godly, pious

die Frömmigkeit godliness,
    piety

die Frucht(ü/e) fruit

fruchtbar fruitful, fertile

die Fruchtbarkeit fruitfulness,
    fertility

früh   early
fühlen   to feel
führen   to lead
der Führer(-)   leader; guide
die Führung   leading, guidance
fünf   five
für (+acc.)   for
furchtbar   frightful(ly)
der Fürst (all other cases -en)
   (reigning) prince
der Fuss(ü/e)   foot

G

ganz (adj.)   whole; (adv.)
   quite, altogether
gar nicht   not at all
die Gattung(en)   genre, kind
gebären (insep.)(p.p.
   geboren)   to bear
   (a child)
das Gebein(e)   bones
geben (pres. gibt; imp. gab;
   p.p. gegeben)   to give
   es gibt (+acc.)   there is/
   are
das Gebet(e)   prayer
das Gebiet(e)   district, region;
   field (of activity,
   thought, etc.)
das Gebilde(-)   thing formed or
   made
geboren   born (see Lesson
   XIV, note a)
das Gebot(e)   commandment
der Gebrauch(äu/e)   use, usage
gebräuchlich   customary(ly),
   usual(ly)
die Geburt(en)   birth
der Gedanke (gen. -ns; all other
   cases -n)   thought
das Gefängnis(se)   prison
gegen (+acc.)   against
gegeneinander   against one
   another
die Gegenreformation   Counter-
   Reformation
der Gegenstand(ä/e)   object
gegenständlich   objective(ly),
   in objective form
gegenüber (+dat.)   opposite;
   in face of
die Gegenwart   present (time);
   presence
gegenwärtig   present
geheim   secret(ly)

das Geheimnis(se)   secret
gehen (imp. ging; p.p. gegangen)
   to go, walk
der Gehorsam   obedience
gehorsam gegen (+acc.)   obedient
   to
der Geist(er)   spirit; mind, intellect
geistig   intellectual
geistlich   spiritual
der Geistliche(n)(declines as
   adj.)   clergyman
gelangen (insep.) zu (+dat.)
   to arrive at, attain
gelegentlich   occasional-
   (ly)
gelehrt   learned, scho-
   larly
geliebt   beloved
gelingen (p.p. gelungen)
   to succeed
   es gelingt (+dat.)   (I)
   succeed
gelten (pres. gilt)   to be
   valid; to apply; to
   count for
gelten für (+acc.)   to be
   considered as
sich geltend machen   to make
   oneself felt, come
   into one's own
die Geltung   validity, force
das Gelüst(e)   desire; lust
gemein   common, mean
die Gemeinde(n)   congrega-
   tion; local church;
   the church (univer-
   sal, etc.); community
die Gemeinschaft   fellowship,
   communion
das Gemüt(er)   nature, disposition, heart
   mit ganzem Gemüt   with
   one's whole being
gemütlich   cosy, snug;
   friendly, convivial;
   good-natured
genug   enough
genügen   to suffice
genügend   sufficient(ly)
gerade (adj.)   straight;
   direct; (adv.) pre-
   cisely, just
gerecht   righteous, just;
   fair
die Gerechtigkeit   righteous-
   ness; fairness

das Gericht(e) judgment; law-court
gering meagre; unimportant
gern gladly, willingly
gesámt total, whole, entire
geschehen (insep.) to happen, come to pass
die Geschichte(n) history; story
geschichtlich historical
das Geschöpf(e) creature
das Gesétz(e) law
gesétzlich legal
das Gesicht(er) face
unter dem Gesichtspunkte (+gen.) from the point of view of
die Gesinnung disposition; character, outlook; conviction
die Gestált(en) shape, form, figure
gestálten (insep.) to fashion, form
gewinnen (p.p. gewónnen) to win; acquire, obtain, gain
gewiss certain
die Gewissheit certainty
gewöhnlich usual(ly)
der Gipfel(-) peak, summit
der Glaube (gen. -ns; all other cases -n) faith, belief
glauben an (+acc.) to believe in
das Glaubensbekénntnis(se) creed, confession of faith
die Glaubenslehre(n) doctrine; dogmatics; doctrinal system
gláubig believing
der Gláubige (declines as adj.) believer
gleich (adj.) equal; same; (adv.) immediately
das Gleichnis(se) parable
gléich/setzen (sep.) to equate
gléichzeitig simultaneous(ly), at the same time
das Glied(er) limb; member; link
die Gnade grace
gnädig gracious
(der)Gott(ö/er) God; god
der Góttesbegriff(e) concept of God
das Góttesbild(er) representation of God

der Góttesdienst(e) (church) service
die Gótteserkénntnis knowledge of God
die Góttesgebärerin 'God-bearer', Mother of God
göttlich divine
der Götze(n) idol
greifbar tangible, palpable
Griechenland Greece
griechisch Greek (adj. and the Greek language)
gross great; big
der Grund(ü/e) reason; ground, cause
auf Grund (+gen.) on the basis of
im Grunde (genommen) at bottom, basically
sich gründen to base oneself
die Gründlage(n) basis, foundation
gründliegend basic, foundational
der Grundsatz(ä/e) principle
die Gründung founding, foundation
die Gruppe(n) group
die Gunst favour
gut (adj.) good; (adv.) well
die Güte kindness
gütig good, gracious, kind

H

die Habe property
haben (pres. hat; imp. hatte; p.p. gehabt) to have
halten (pres. hält) to hold, keep; to halt
die Hand(ä/e) hand
handeln an (+dat.) to act towards
die Handlung(en) shop; action
hart hard
hassen to hate
das Haupt(äu/er) head; (in compounds) main, chief
das Haus(äu/er) house
der Hebräer(-) Hebrew
hebräisch Hebrew (adj. and the Hebrew language)
das Heft(e) booklet; issue, 'number' (of periodical)

der Heide (all other cases -n)
    heathen, pagan
heidnisch heathen, pagan
das Heil salvation; (as greet-
    ing) hail!
der Heiland Saviour
heilig holy
heiligen to sanctify,
    hallow
die Heiligung sanctification
die Heilsgeschichte history of
    salvation
heilsnotwendig necessary for
    salvation
héim/kehren (sep.) to go
    home
héim/suchen (sep.) to visit
    (with judgment, etc.)
die Héimsuchung(en) visitation,
    affliction
heissen to be called; to mean;
    to be stated
  das heisst (d.h.) that is,
    i.e.
her (see Lesson XII, note q)
herán/treten (sep.)(pres.
    tritt) to draw near,
    come towards
heráus/geben (sep.)(p.p. heráus-
    gegeben)(herausg.) to
    edit
heráus/nehmen (sep.) to take
    out
herbéi/führen (sep.) to bring
    about, give rise to
die Herde(n) herd, flock
der Herr (other sing. cases -n;
    all pl. cases -en) Lord;
    gentleman; Mr
das Herrenwort(e) dominical
    saying
herrlich magnificent;
    glorious
die Herrlichkeit magnificence;
    glory
herrschen to rule, hold sway;
    to prevail
der Herrscher(-) ruler, sovereign
hervór/gehen (sep.)(p.p. gegan-
    gen) to emerge, proceed
hervór/heben (sep.)(imp. hob;
    p.p. gehoben) to empha-
    size, bring into promi-
    nence
hervórragend eminent, salient
hervór/rufen (sep.) to call
    forth

das Herz (gen. -ens; dat., all pl.
    cases -en) heart
Hesékiel Ezekiel
hier here
hierán to this
hierdúrch through this, by
    means of this
die Hilfe help, aid
hilfreich helpful
der Himmel(-) sky; heaven
die Himmelfahrt ascension;
    assumption
hináus/stossen (sep.) (imp.
    stiess; p.p. gestossen)
    to cast out, thrust out,
    expel
hinéin/gehen (sep.) to go in
hinéin/gehören (sep.) in
    (+acc.) to belong in
hinéin/legen (sep.) in (+acc.)
    to attribute to
hinéin/lesen (sep.) in (+acc.)
    to read into
die Hingabe surrender
die Hinsicht(en) view, respect
  in dieser Hinsicht in this
    respect
hinter behind
der Hínweis(e) auf (+acc.) refe-
    rence to
hín/weisen (sep.) auf (+acc.)
    to refer to
der Hirte (all other cases -n)
    shepherd
hoch (drops c in declension)
    high, tall
höchst (superlative of hoch)
    (adj.) highest; (adv.)
    most
hoffen auf (+acc.) to hope
    for
die Hoffnung(en) hope
die Hölle hell
hören to hear
der Hörer(-) hearer
die Huld grace, favour
die Hülle(n) veil; cover
hungrig hungry

I

ich I
die Idée(n) idea
ihm (dat. of er; es) (to)
    him; (to) it
ihn (acc. of er) him, it

Vocabulary

ihnen (<u>dat.</u> of sie, pl.)
(to) them
Ihnen (<u>dat.</u> of Sie) (to)
you (polite form)
ihr (2nd pl. pronoun) you
(familiar form, pl.)
ihr (<u>dat.</u> of sie, sing.)
(to) her
ihr (poss. adj. of sie, sing.
and of sie, pl.) her;
their
Ihr (poss. adj. of Sie)
your (polite form)
immer always, ever
immer wieder ever again,
again and again
indém (conj.) while, since,
as; in that
das Individuum (pl. Individuen)
individual
der Inhalt content(s)
innen inside
nach innen inwards
das Innere (declines as adj.)
inward part(s)
innerlich inward
insbesóndere in particular
interessánt interesting
irdisch earthly
irgend ein (sing.) any ...
(at all)
irgend welche (pl.) any ...
(at all)
isolíeren to isolate
ist (3rd sing. pres. of sein)
is

J

ja yes (see Lesson XV, note <u>e</u>)
das Jahr(e) year
das Jahrhúndert(e) century
je ever
je nach Wunsch as desired
jédenfalls at any rate,
in any case
jeder (declines like definite
article) each, every
jedoch yet, nevertheless,
however
jemand someone, anyone
jener (declines like definite
article) that, those
Jesája Isaiah
jetzt now
der Jude (all other cases -<u>n</u>) Jew

das Judentum Jewry; Judaism
die Júdin(nen) Jewess
jüdisch Jewish
die Jugend youth; young people
der Júnger(-) disciple
die Jura(pl.) law (academic discipline)
der Juríst (all other cases -<u>en</u>)
lawyer

K

kalt cold
das Kapítel(-) chapter
kaum scarcely, hardly
der Kegel(-) skittle
kein not a, no, not any
kennen (imp. <u>kannte</u>) to
know, be acquainted
with
kennen/lernen (sep.) to get
to know, learn to know
der Kenner(-) one who knows,
connoisseur
das Kénnzeichen(-) mark, characteristic
das Kind(er) child
das Kindlein(-) little child
kindlich childlike
die Kirche(n) church
die Kirchenzucht church discipline
kirchlich ecclesiastical
die Klage(n) complaint
klar clear
klein small, little
das Kloster(ö) monastery; con-
vent
der Knabe (all other cases -<u>n</u>)
boy
der Knecht(e) servant
kommen (imp. <u>kam</u>; p.p. <u>gekommen</u>)
to come
komplizíeren to complicate
der König(e) king
die Königin(en) queen
konkrét concrete
können (pres. <u>kann</u>; imp.
<u>konnte</u>) to be able,
'can'
konzipíeren to conceive
(idea, etc.)
der Kopf(ö/e) head
der Körper(-) body
körperlich bodily, physical-
(ly)

die Kraft(ä/e) power; strength
kräftig powerful, strong
krank ill, sick
die Krankheit(en) illness, sick-
　　ness
kreatürlich creaturely
das Kreuz(e) cross
kreuzigen to crucify
die Kreuzigung(en) crucifixion
kriegen to get, obtain
kühn daring, bold
kurz short, brief(ly)
die Kurzatmigkeit shortage of
　　breath; breathless im-
　　patience

L

das Lamm(ä/er) lamb
das Land(ä/er) land, country;
　　countryside, state
der Landsmann (pl. Landsleute)
　　fellow-countryman
lassen (pres. lässt; imp.
　　lieos) to leave, let,
　　allow; cause (see Lesson
　　XI, note e)
lau lukewarm
laufen (pres. läuft) to run
launisch capricious
die Laxheit laxity
leben to live
das Leben life
lebendig alive, living;
　　lively
lebenskräftig vigorous,
　　vital
leer empty
legen to lay, put down; to
　　impose
das Lehramt(ä/er) teaching
　　office; magisterium
lehramtlich of the magi-
　　sterium
das Lehrbuch (ü/er) text-book
die Lehre(n) teaching, doctrine
lehren to teach
der Lehrer(-) teacher
der Leib(er) body; belly
leiblich bodily, physical
das Leid grief, trouble; harm,
　　injury
leiden to suffer
das Leiden suffering; passion
　　(of Christ)

die Leistung(en) achievement
leiten to direct, conduct,
　　manage
die Lektüre reading
lernen to learn; to study
lesen to read
der Leser(-) reader
letzt last
letzten Endes in the final
　　analysis
letzteres the latter
leugnen to deny
der Leugner(-) denier
die Leute (pl.) people
das Licht(er) light
lieb dear, beloved
lieb haben to love, hold
　　dear
die Liebe love
lieben to love
lieblich lovely
das Lied(er) song
liegen to lie
liegen an (+dat.) to depend
　　on
die Lösung(en) solution

M

machen to make, do
die Macht(ä/e) power, might
mächtig powerful, mighty
mag (see mögen)
das Mahl(e) meal
die Majestät majesty
majestätisch majestic
der Makel(-) stain, blemish
das Mal(e) time, i.e. occasion
　　(see Lesson X, note c)
man one; 'they', 'you', etc.
　　(see Lesson XII, note m)
manch many a; a good number
　　of
der Mangel an (+dat.) lack of
der Mann(ä/er) man; husband
das Mass(e) amount; measure
das Meer(e) sea
mehr more
mein my
meinen to think; to mean;
　　to say
meiner (gen. of ich) of me
die Meinung(en) opinion
der Mensch (all other cases -en)
　　human being; person; man;
　　mankind

menschlich   human
der Messías   Messiah
    metaéthisch   superethical
    mich (acc. of ich)   me
die Mílderung   softening, toning
        down
    mir (dat. of ich)   (to) me
    misslich   dangerous, perilous
    mit (+dat.)   with
    mit/empfinden (sep.)   to feel
        in common
    mit/geben (p.p. gegeben)   to
        give along with; to imply
        (see Lesson XV, note b)
das Mitglied(er)   member
der Mitknecht(e)   fellow-servant
das Mítleiden   fellow-suffering;
        sympathy
die Mitte   middle
das Mittel(-)   means
das Mittelalter   Middle Ages
    mittelalterlich   medieval
    mittels (+gen.)   by means of
die Mittelstellung(en)   middle
        position
    mitten in (+dat.)   in the
        midst of
    mögen (pres. mag; imp. mochte)
        to like; 'may' (possibly)
    möglich   possible
die Möglichkeit(en)   possibility
    möglichst   as far as possible
der Mönch(e)   monk
    mönchisch   monastic
der Mord   murder
der Mörder(-)   murderer
der Morgen(-)   morning
    München   Munich
der Mund(e)   mouth
    müssen (pres. muss; imp.
        musste)   to have to,
        'must'
die Mutter(ü)   mother
    mütterlich   motherly, maternal
die Mýstik   mysticism
der Mýstiker(-)   mystic
    mýstisch   mystical

N

    nach (+dat.)   after; accor-
        ding to
    nach aussen   outwards
    nach Christo   A.D.
    nach innen   inwards

die Náchfolge Christi   imitation
        of Christ
    nách/jagen (sep.)(+dat.)   to
        chase after
    nách/lassen (sep.)(p.p. gelas-
        sen)   to leave behind;
        (p.p.)   posthumous
die Nacht(ä/e)   night
    nackt   naked
    nah(e)   near
    näher (comparative of nah)
        nearer; more precise
sich nähern (+dat.)   to approach;
        to get nearer
der Name (gen. -ns; all other
        cases -n)   name
    námentlich   especially
    nämlich   namely; you see
der Narr (all other cases -en)
        fool
    zum Narren halten   make (a)
        fool(s) of
die Natúr   nature
    natúrlich   natural(ly); of
        course
    nehmen (imp. nahm; p.p. genom-
        men)   to take
    nein   no
    nennen (p.p. genannt)   to name,
        call
    neu   new
der Neutestaméntler(-)   N.T.
        scholar
    neutestaméntlich   N.T. (adj.)
die Neuzeit   recent times
    nicht   not
    nichts   nothing; not at all
    nie(mals)   never
    níeder/fallen (sep.)(imp. fiel)
        to fall down
die Níederlande(pl.)   the Nether-
        lands
    niemand   no-one
    nirgends   nowhere
    noch   still, yet; nor; more
    noch einmal   once more
    noch nicht   not yet
die Not(ö/e)   distress, trouble;
        emergency, need
    nötigen   to oblige, necessi-
        tate, compel
    nót/tun (+dat.)   to be needful
        for
    nun   now
    nur   only

O

ob   whether
obschón   although
obwóhl   although
oder   or
offen   open
óffenbar   manifest, evident
offenbáren   to reveal
offenbárt   revealed
die Offenbárung(en)   revelation;
    Apocalypse
óffenkundig   widely known,
    manifest
oft   often, frequently
ohne (+acc.)   without
ohne weiteres   without further
    ado
das Ohr(en)   ear
ökuménisch   ecumenical
das Opfer(-)   sacrifice, offering
opfern   to sacrifice, offer
der Opfertod   sacrificial death
der Orden(-)   order (monastic,
    etc.)
der Órdenstand   being in the or-
    der
die Órdnung(en)   order; ordinance
der Ort(e)   place

P

der Papst(ä/e)   pope
päpstlich   papal
die Partéi(en)   party
die Pflege   care, fostering
pflegen   to care for, foster,
    look after
pietétisch   pietistic
pietístisch   pietistic; sanc-
    timonious
plötzlich   sudden(ly)
prédigen   to preach
die Prédiger(-)   preacher
die Predigt(en)   sermon
der Preis(e)   prize; price
die Préisgabe   surrender
der Priester(-)   priest
priésterlich   priestly
der Prophét(en)   prophet
prüfen   to test, check
die Prüfung(en)   examination
der Punkt(e)   point; dot, full
    stop

Q

die Quelle(n)   source

R

der Rahmen(-)   frame
ráhmenlos   without a frame,
    unframed
der Raum(äu/e)   room; space,
    place
im Raume (+gen.)   within
    the sphere of
rechnen   to count, reckon
recht   right; real(ly), true,
    proper(ly)
das Recht(e)   right; law; recti-
    tude
mit Recht   with good cause,
    justly
réchtfertigen   to justify
die Réchtfertigung   justification
rechtgláubig   orthodox
die Réchtgläubigkeit   orthodoxy
die Rede(n)   speech; address;
    words
reden   to talk
reduzíeren auf (+acc.)   to
    reduce to
der Reformátor (pl. Reformatóren)
    reformer
reformatórisch   reforming; of
    the Reformers
reformíeren   to reform
die Regel(n)   rule
regíeren   to rule, reign
das Reich(e)   kingdom; empire
die Reihe(n)   row, rank, line;
    strand
rein   pure; clean
die Réinigung   purification
reisen   to travel, journey
rennen   to run; to race
der Rest(e)   remainder; remnant,
    vestige
die Reue   repentance; regret
reuen   to regret, repent
es reut mich   I regret it
richten an (+acc.)   to direct
    to
der Richter(-)   judge
richtig   correct(ly), right-
    (ly)
rivalisíeren   to rival,
    compete

Rom   Rome
der Römer(-)   Roman
römisch   Roman (adj.)
der Ruf(e)   call, cry; reputation;
 calling
rufen (imp. <u>rief</u>)   to call,
 shout
die Ruhe   calm, quiet

S

die Sache(n)   thing; affair,
 matter
sagen   to say; to tell
salben   to anoint
die Salbung   anointing; unction
die Sammlung(en)   collection
die Satzung(en)   statute
der Schaden   harm, damage
das Schaf(e)   sheep
schaffen (imp. <u>schuf</u>)   to
 create
der Schatz(ä/e)   treasure
die Schau(en)   **survey, review**
schauen   to look
scheiden (imp. <u>schied</u>)   to
 separate, divide; to
 divorce
scheinen (imp. <u>schien</u>)   to
 seem; to shine
die Schilderung(en)   depiction,
 portrayal
schlie<u>ss</u>en (imp. <u>schloss</u>)
 to close, shut
schlie<u>ss</u>en auf (+<u>acc.</u>)
 to deduce, come to con-
 clusions about
schliesslich   finally, at
 last
der Schluss(ü/e)   end; conclusion
 den Schluss ziehen   to
 draw the conclusion
schneiden (imp. <u>schnitt</u>)   to
 cut
die Scholástik   scholasticism
der Scholástiker   schoolman
schon   already
der Schöpfer(-)   creator
die Schöpfung   creation
schrecklich   fearful, terri-
 ble
schreiben (imp. <u>schrieb</u>; p.p.
 <u>geschrieben</u>)   to write
schreien (imp. <u>schrie</u>)   to
 cry, shout, yell

die Schrift(en)   scripture;
 writing; (literary) work;
 periodical
die Schuld(en)   guilt; debt;
 fault
schuldig   guilty; in debt
das Schuldopfer(-)   guilt-offering
schweben   to hover; to soar
die Seele(n)   soul
der Segen(-)   blessing
segnen   to bless
sehen (pres. <u>sieht</u>; imp. <u>sah</u>;
 p.p. <u>gesehen</u>)   to see;
 to look, behold
sehr   very; very much
sei (2nd sing. imperative of
 sein)   be!
 ich, er sei (1st and 3rd
 sing. pres. subjunctive
 of sein)   (let me) be,
 (let him) be
ihr seid (2nd pl. pres.
 tense of sein)   ye are
sein (infinitive)   to be
sein (possessive adj.)   his,
 its
die Seite(n)   page; side
 auf Seiten (+<u>gen.</u>)   on the
 part of
selber   -self (see Lesson
 VII, note <u>e</u>)
selbst   -self (see Lesson
 VII, note <u>e</u>)
die Selbstherrlichkeit   self-
 glorification
selig   blessed; overjoyed;
 in heaven; finally saved;
 late, deceased
selten   rare(ly), seldom
senden (p.p. <u>gesandt</u>)   to send
setzen   to put, place, set
sich (3rd person reflexive pronoun, <u>acc.</u> or <u>dat.</u>)   (to)
 himself, herself, itself,
 oneself, themselves;
 (yourself)
die Sicherheit   certainty; safety;
 complacency
die Sicht(en)   view
sichtbar   visible
sie (3rd person pronoun, sing.
 (fem.) and pl. <u>nom.</u> or
 <u>acc.</u>)   she, her; they,
 them
Sie (takes 3rd person pl. verb)
 (<u>nom.</u> or <u>acc.</u>)   you (polite form)

sieben(mal) seven (times)
der Sieg(e) victory
siehe! behold! lo!
sie sind they are
wir sind we are
singen to sing
der Sinn(e) meaning, sense
sinnlich sensual
sinnlos senseless
sinnvoll meaningful
die Sitte(n) custom
die Sittenlehre ethics
sittlich moral
der Sitz(e) seat
Sitz im Leben life-setting
so so; in this way; like
   this
sogar even
der Sohn(ö/e) son
solch such
sollen (pres. soll) to
   be supposed to; 'shall',
   'is to'
somit thus, consequently
sondern (used only after a
   negative) but (on the
   contrary)
sonst otherwise; further, in
   addition
sorgen für (+acc.) to care
   for, look after
spät late
das Spielzeug(e) plaything, toy
die Spitze(n) tip, point
die Sprache(n) speech; language
zur Sprache kommen to be
   put into words; to be
   discussed, talked about
sprechen (pres. spricht;
   imp. sprach; p.p. ge-
   sprochen) to speak; to
   say
der Spruch(ü/e) proverb; saying
die Stadt(ä/e) town, city
stammen aus (+dat.) to ori-
   ginate from
standhaft steadfast, steady
ständig constant(ly)
stark strong(ly)
statt (+gen.) instead of
stehen to stand
stehlen to steal
sich steigern to increase, inten-
   sify
der Stein(e) stone
steinern stone, of stone

die Stelle(n) place; position;
   passage
an seiner Stelle in his
   place; in place of him
stellen to place, put
sterben (p.p. gestorben) to
   die
sterblich mortal
der Stern(e) star
die Stimme(n) voice
der Stoff(e) substance, material
die Strafe(n) punishment
strafen to punish
die Straffähigkeit punishabi-
   lity
das Stück(e) piece; item
studieren to study
der Studierende (declines as
   adj.) student
das Studium (pl. Studien)
   study; university
   course
die Stufe(n) step; degree, rank
stumm dumb
suchen to seek, look for,
   attempt
die Sünde(n) sin
der Sünder(-) sinner
sündhaft sinful
sündigen to sin
sündlos sinless
die Szene(n) scene
in Szene setzen to bring
   into view; to enact,
   perform

T

der Tag(e) day
die Tat(en) deed, act
in der Tat indeed, in fact
der Täter(-) doer; culprit
tätig active
die Tätigkeit activity
die Tatsache(n) fact
tatsächlich in fact,
   really
taub deaf
der Teil(e) part
die Tendenz zu (+dat.) tendency
   to
der Terminus (pl. Termini) term
der Teufel(-) devil
tief deep

Vocabulary

die Tiefe(n)   the deep; depth
der Tisch(e)   table
der Titel(-)   title
die Tochter(ö)   daughter
der Tod   death
   toll   crazy, mad
der Ton(ö/e)   tone, sound
der Ton(e)   clay
der Töpfer(-)   potter
das Tor(e)   gate
   tot   dead
   töten   to kill
   tragen (pres. trägt)   to
      carry; to bear; to wear
der Traktát(e)   tract, treatise
   tränken   to give drink to
   trennen   to separate
   treu(lich)   faithful(ly),
      true
der Trost   comfort, consolation
   trösten   to comfort, console
   tröstlich   comforting
   trotz (+gen.; occasionally
      +dat.)   in spite of
   tückisch   capricious,
      spiteful
die Tugend(en)   virtue
   tugendhaft   virtuous
   tun (imp. tat; p.p. getan)
      to do
die Tür(en)   door

U

   über (+acc.)   over, across;
      about; (+dat.)   over,
      above
   überáll   everywhere
   überáus   extremely
   überéin/stimmen (sep.)   to
      agree, concur, be unani-
      mous
   überflüssig   superfluous,
      abundant
   überháupt   at all; in general
   überlássen (insep.)   to leave
   uns selbst überlássen (p.p.)
      left to ourselves
die Überlíeferung   tradition
der Übermut   arrogance, presump-
      tion
   übernéhmen (insep.)   to take
      over
   übersétzen (insep.)   to trans
      late
die Übersétzung(en)   translation

   überwínden (insep.)   to over-
      come, conquer
die Überwíndung   conquest
   überzéugen (insep.)   to con-
      vince
   üblich   usual, customary
die Übung(en)   exercise; prac-
      tice
   um (+acc.)   around
   um euretwillen   for your
      sakes
   um so (+comparative)   all the
      more
   um (+gen.) willen   for the
      sake of
   um ... zu (+infinitive)   in
      order to
der Umgang   acquaintance, associa-
      tion
   umgében (insep.)   to surround
   úm/gehen (sep.) mit (+dat.)
      to deal with, treat
die Úmkehr   conversion, turning
      back
die Umsetzung   transposition
   únangemessen   inappropriate
   únbefleckt   immaculate,
      unsullied
   únberührbar   untouchable
die Únbotmássigkeit   insubor-
      dination
   und   and
   und so weiter (u.s.w.)
      and so on, etc.
   únehelich   out of wedlock,
      illegitimate
   únerforschlich   unfathom-
      able
   úngeheuer   enormous
der Úngehorsam   disobedience
   úngekürzt   unabbreviated
die Úngerechtigkeit   unrighteous-
      ness; injustice, unfair-
      ness
der Únglaube (gen. -ns; other
      cases -n)   unbelief
   úngleich   unequal
   únglücklicherweise   unfor-
      tunately
das Únheil   perdition; disaster
das Únrecht   wrong
   Únrecht tun (+dat.)   to do
      wrong to
   únrein   impure
die Únreinheit   impurity, unclean-
      ness

die Unruhe agitation, unrest,
   disquiet
   uns (acc. and dat. of wir)
      us, (to) us
die Unschuld innocence
   unschuldig innocent
   unser our
   unsterblich immortal
   unter (+acc. or dat.) under;
      among
   unterlassen (insep.) to fail,
      omit
   unter/legen (sep.)(+dat.) to
      attribute to, ascribe to
   unterscheiden (insep.) to
      distinguish, differen-
      tiate
die Unterscheidung(en) differen-
      tiation
der Unterschied(e) difference
   unter/stellen (sep.)(+dat.)
      to subordinate to,
      subject to
die Untersuchung(en) examina-
      tion, enquiry
   unterweisen (insep.)(p.p.
      unterwiesen) to teach,
      instruct
die Unterweisung instruction
   unvermeidlich unavoidable,
      inevitable
   unverwüstlich indestructi-
      ble, imperturbable
die Unwissenheit ignorance
die Unzier blemish, disfigurement
   unzugänglich inaccessible,
      unapproachable
   urchristlich early Christian
das Urteil(e) judgment; sentence
   urteilen to judge; to form
      a judgment

V

der Vater(ä) father
   väterlich fatherly, paternal
die Verachtung contempt
   verändern (insep.) to change,
      alter
die Veränderung(en) change,
      alteration
   veranstalten (insep.) to
      arrange, organize, bring
      about
   verantwortlich responsible,
      answerable

die Verantwortung responsibility
   verbergen (insep.)(p.p. verbor-
      gen) to conceal, hide
   verbieten (insep.)(p.p. ver-
      boten) to forbid,
      prohibit
   verbinden (insep.)(p.p. ver-
      bunden) to link,
      connect
die Verbindung(en) link, con-
      nection
die Verborgenheit hiddenness
das Verbot(e) prohibition
   verdunkeln (insep.) to
      obscure, darken
   verehren (insep.) to
      venerate, revere
die Verehrung veneration
   vereinigen (insep.) to
      unite
die Vereinigung(en) union
   verfahren (insep.) to pro-
      ceed
das Verfahren(-) process, pro-
      cedure
   verfluchen (insep.) to
      curse
   verfolgen (insep.) to
      persecute
die Verfolgung(en) persecution
   vergeben (insep.)(+dat.)
      to forgive
die Vergebung forgiveness
   vergehen (insep.) to pass
      away
   vergleichen (insep.) to
      compare
das Verhalten behaviour
das Verhältnis(se) relation-
      ship
   verhärten (insep.) to
      harden
die Verheissung(en) promise
   verknüpfen (insep.) to
      link
   verkünd(ig)en (insep.)
      to preach, proclaim
die Verkündigung preaching,
      proclamation
der Verlag publishing house
   verlassen (insep.) to
      leave, quit; to abandon
die Verlassenheit abandoned
      state; dereliction
der Verlauf course
   verlieren (insep.)(p.p. ver-
      loren) to lose

Vocabulary

sich vermählen (insep.) to
    marry
die Vermittlung instrumental-
    ity
    vermögen (insep.)(pres.
        vermag; imp. vermochte)
        to be able to
    vermutlich presumably,
        probably
    vernehmen (insep.) to
        hear; to perceive
die Vernunft reason, intellect
    vernünftig rational,
        reasonable
die Verpflichtung(en) obliga-
        tion
der Vers(e) verse
    verschaffen (insep.) to
        provide, supply
    verschieden different;
        various
    verschlingen (insep.) to
        swallow up
    versehen (insep.)(p.p.
        versehen) to provide
    versetzen (insep.) to
        displace
    versiegeln (insep.) to
        seal up
    versöhnen (insep.) to re-
        concile
die Versöhnung reconciliation
der Verstand understanding,
        intelligence
das Verständnis understanding,
        appreciation
    verstehen (insep.)(imp.
        verstand; p.p. verstan-
        den) to understand
    verstehen unter (+dat.) to
        understand by
die Verstockung hardness of
        heart
    versuchen (insep.) to try,
        attempt; to tempt
die Versuchung(en) temptation
    verteidigen (insep.) to
        defend
das Vertrauen auf (+acc.)
        reliance on, confidence
        in
    vertreten (insep.)(pres.
        vertritt; p.p. vertre-
        ten) to represent;
        to uphold, advocate
        (opinion, etc.)

    verurteilen (insep.) to
        condemn
    vervollständigen (insep.)
        to complete, fill out
die Verwahrlosung neglect
    verweisen (insep.) auf (+acc.)
        to refer to
    verwenden (insep.) to use
die Verwerfung rejection; re-
        probation
    verwiesen (p.p. of verweisen)
        auf (+acc.) dependent
        on
    verzweifeln (insep.) to
        despair
die Verzweiflung despair
    viel(es) much, a lot; (pl.)
        many
    vielleicht perhaps
    vielmehr rather
    vier four
das Volk("ö/er) people, nation
    voll full(y), -ful
    völlig complete(ly)
die Vollkommenheit perfection;
        completeness
    von (+dat.) of; from; by
    von ... ab from ... onwards
    von ... aus from; starting
        from
    von ... her from; origi-
        nating from
    voneinander from one
        another
    vor (+acc. or dat.) in front
        of; before
    vor allem above all, espe-
        cially
    vor Christo B.C.
    voraus/setzen (sep.) to
        assume, presuppose
die Voraussetzung(en) assump-
        tion, presupposition
der Vorbehalt reservation,
        proviso
    nicht ohne den Vorbehalt
        (+gen.) without preju-
        dice to
    unter Vorbehalt (+gen.)
        without prejudice to
das Vorbild(er) model, pattern
    vor/gehen (sep.) to proceed
das Vorgehen procedure, pro-
        gress, action
der Vorgesetzte (declines as adj.)
        superior

der Vórhalt   remonstrance, re-
       proach
die Vorhérbestimmung   fore-
       ordination, predestina-
       tion
die Vórsehung   providence
das Vórurteil(e)   prejudice
   vórwiegend   predominant(ly)
   vór/ziehen (sep.)   to prefer

                W

   wachsen   to grow
das Wachstum   growth
der Wächter(-)   watchman
   wählen   to choose
   wahr   true
   während (prep.)(+gen.)
       during; (conj.) while
   wáhrhaftig   truthful
lie Wáhrheit   truth
   wáhrlich   truly, verily
   wáhrnehmbar   perceivable,
       perceptible
   wáhr/nehmen (sep.)   to
       perceive
der Wandel   walk, walking
   wandeln   to walk
die Wandlung(en)   transfor-
       mation, change
   wann (used in direct or re-
       ported questions)
       when
   war   (see sein, 'to be')
   ward   (archaic imperfect
       of werden)
die Wärme   warmth, heat
   warnen   to warn
   warúm   why
   was   what; (relative pro-
       noun)   that
das Wasser   water
die Wéchselbeziehung   mutual
       relation
   weder ... noch   neither
       ... nor
der Weg(e)(e pron. long)   way;
       path; road
   wég/fallen (sep.)(e pron.
       short)   to fall away
   weil   because
   weise   wise
die Weise(n)   manner, way,
       aspect
   auf diese Weise   in this
       manner

die Weisheit   wisdom
   weiss   white
   weiss   (see wissen)
die Wéissagung(en)   prophecy
die Weisung(en)   direction
   weit(er)   far(ther)
       und so weiter (u.s.w.)
         and so on, etc.
   wéiter/entwickeln (sep.)
       to develop further
   wéitschichtig   immense, vast
   welcher (declines like definite
       article)   which; some,
       any
die Welle(n)   wave
die Welt(en)   world
   wem (dat. of wer, 'who')   to
       whom
die Wende(n)   turn-about; turning-
       point
sich wenden   to turn; to address
       oneself
die Wendung(en)   turning
   wenig(e)   little, not much;
       (pl.)   few
   wenn   if; when; whenever
   wenn ... auch   even if
   wer   who; he who
   werden (pres. wird; imp. wurde;
       p.p. geworden)   to
       become; (future tense)
       will; shall; (passive
       voice)   be
   werfen (imp. warf)   to throw;
       to cast
das Werk(e)   work; piece of work
   wert   worth; worthy
der Wert(e)   worth, value
das Wesen(-)   being; creature;
       essence, nature
   wésentlich   essential(ly)
   wichtig   important
die Wíchtigkeit   importance
   wider (+acc.)   against, con-
       trary to
   widerspréchen (insep.)(+dat.)
       to contradict
   wie   how; as, like
   wieder   again
die Wiederáufrichtung   resto-
       ration
die Wíedergabe   reproduction;
       likeness
   wíeder/kommen (sep.)   to come
       back, return
die Wíederkunft   return; (of
       Christ) Second Coming,

Second Advent

wieweit   how far

der Wille (gen. -ns; all other cases -n)   will

die Willkür   free will; arbitrariness

willkürlich   despotic; arbitrary

wir   we

wirken   to act, work; to effect, produce

das Wirken   working, activity

wirklich   real(ly)

die Wirklichkeit   reality

wissen (pres. weiss; imp. wusste)   to know

das Wissen um (+acc.)   knowledge of, about

wissen zu (+infinitive)   to know how to

die Wissenschaft(en)   science; scholarship

wissenschaftlich   scientific; scholarly

wo   where

die Woche(n)   week

die Woge(n)   billow

wohin   where to, whither

wohl   probably; well

wohnen   to dwell, live

die Wohnung(en)   dwelling; abode; house; flat

wollen (pres. will)   to want (to); to intend to

das Wort(e)   word

wörtlich   literal(ly); verbal(ly)

das Wunder(-)   wonder; miracle

wunderbar   wonderful; miraculous

der Wunsch(ü/e)   wish, desire

würdig   worthy

wüst   desolate, waste

die Wüste(n)   desert, wilderness

Z

zählen zu (+dat.)   to count, reckon among

zahlreich   numerous

das Zeichen(-)   sign

zeigen   to show

sich zeigen   to be seen, appear

die Zeit(en)   time; period

zu allen Zeiten   at all times

zu jeder Zeit   at all times; at any time

das Zeitalter(-)   era, epoch, period

die Zeitschrift(en)   periodical, magazine, journal

zerreissen (insep.)(p.p. zerrissen)   to break; to tear in pieces

zersplittern (insep.)   to split up

die Zerstörung   destruction, overthrow

zerstreuen (insep.)   to disperse

die Zerstreuung   dispersal, dispersion

der Zeuge(n)   witness

zeugen   to witness; to beget

das Zeugnis   testimony

Zeugnis ablegen   to testify

die Zeugung   begetting, procreation

ziehen (imp. zog; p.p. gezogen)(intransitive) to move; (transitive) to pull

das Ziel(e)   aim, goal

die Zier or Zierde(n)   adornment, ornament

zieren   to adorn, embellish

der Zögling(e)   pupil

der Zorn   anger, wrath

zu (+dat.)   to; at; for the purpose of; too

die Zucht   discipline

züchtigen   to discipline; to chastise

die Züchtigung   chastisement

zugleich   at the same time

zu/kommen (sep.)(+dat.)   to belong to, be appropriate to

die Zukunft   future

zu/lassen (sep.)(p.p. gelassen)   to permit

zum Beispiel (z.B.)   for example, e.g.

zu/muten (sep.)(+dat.)   to expect of

zunächst   first of all; in the first place

zurück/schaudern (sep.)   to shrink back

zurück/treten (sep.)(pres. tritt)   to recede; to step back

Grammatical Index

N.B. Large Roman numerals (I, II, etc.) indicate lessons;
   Arabic numerals (1, 2, etc.) indicate sections in the grammatical
      introductions to Lessons I - X;
   letters (a, b, etc.) indicate sections in the grammatical notes;
   small Roman numerals (i, ii, etc.) indicate sub-sections in the
      grammatical notes.

Index

Index